Thoughts for Transformation

Thoughts for Transformation

Spiritual Insights for Positive Living

LeRoy E. Zemke

THOUGHTS FOR TRANSFORMATION
Spiritual Insights for Positive Living

First Edition

For ordering of additional books, or information, write to:

LeRoy E. Zemke
P.O. Box 12235
St. Petersburg, FL 33733

ISBN 0-9628360-0-1

Cover art and design by ChromaGraphics

A UNIQUE WEEKLY GUIDE
TO SELF EMPOWERMENT FOR INNER PEACE,
FULFILLMENT AND PROSPERITY.

Introduction

Over the past 35 years, I have been actively and intricately involved in a public New Thought, Metaphysical, Interfaith Ministry, the core of which embraces teaching, lecturing and counseling. The focus of this ministry has been at the home church in Florida and has expanded to many areas across the U.S.A. and abroad as well. Within the context of my ministry I am privileged to observe the many, varied human interactions, the intensely emotional, the psychological and spiritual experiences of men, women and children from almost every walk of life. This kind of involvement is a powerful gift and constantly brings me new discernments, discoveries and deeper perceptions regarding the spectra of human interchange and our shared life together.

Metaphysics, as one emerging system of a spiritual teaching, offers expanded and/or different views or options about life. One of its gifts is that it offers us a unique opportunity to look at crisis, challenge, or changes of whatever kind in our lives and enables us to realize that we can glean specific insights and significant learning from our varied experiences. We discover we can absorb positive as well as restrictive components from life. *And that we have choices* about how to view and review or refocus or revision what is happening or what has happened to us in our current life circumstances.

The unique collection of materials within this book emerged over a period of many years, evolving slowly into the form it now comprises. These short inspirational essay style writings, were originally designed for a general readership perceived to be a metaphysically minded, spiritually oriented audience, both at the Temple of the Living God, in St. Petersburg, Florida and the extended "family" of friends and other interested people all across the country as I have met them in my travels as a teacher and consultant.

In writing these materials, special themes were considered: Prosperity, Spiritual Healing, Inner Awareness, Goal Setting, Success, Forgiveness, Spiritual Awakening and Spiritual

Development, Understanding Psychic Awareness, Holistic Health, Creativity, The Nature of Spiritual Reality, and a variety of abbreviated discussions of and upon other metaphysical subjects and approaches to life.

Eventually a 52 Week Guide evolved as a basic structure or plan for this book. Using one theme for one week, the material can be studied and utilized so that the reader will first come to understand its broad nature and content, see or sense the need for or desirability of change and then, within the context of daily living, actually experience the growth or change using the ideas, suggestions and recommendations as a *step by step* process.

Therefore, over the next 52 weeks, take one theme each week and allow yourself to study and reflect upon the material thoroughly. Read it at leisure, or at an unhurried pace and also at an appointed time that is used for internal study and development.

Certain articles offer specific writing tasks to complete or they make practical suggestions concerning ways to go about accomplishing particular objectives. Set aside regular periods for what might be called practice times. Some exercises are brief and may take 10-15 minutes. Others may require several days or a week or longer to accomplish. Give yourself permission to do the suggested work. The benefit will accrue to you as you do the recommended exercises.

There is no special order in which to proceed as far as study of these materials is concerned. You will find certain topics have an immediate personal appeal because of a most unique situation occurring in your life at the moment. Follow your own prompting, in your own way, and read, study and apply the content of that essay, or that section or weekly guide. Results will follow consistent application. Sometimes it may be necessary to repeat, or do the exercise(s) which are offered over again. Initially, when we search for quick answers, results are less complete, less satisfactory. Be patient with your own process of discovery. Be willing to consider the necessary individual pacing of your own personal growth and learning.

Since the essays are intentionally short, some possessing a more poetic rhythm than others, a rapid reading or pursuit of intellectual information or content alone will seldom satisfy. The deepening value will come from a more deliberate, reflective approach when one can allow time for inward viewing, contemplation or just the simple refocusing of one's attitude about some issue, or toward gaining insight regarding a stage of growth, change or spiritual development occurring in one's life.

These weekly guides are written from psychological perspectives as well as ethical viewpoints. Some contain mundane, down to earth, "hands on" do it yourself suggestions to deal with fear, loneliness, hurt and grief. Some offer vision, inspiration and hope. Others suggest spiritual practices such as prayer and/or meditation in old, familiar ways and yet very modern and updated ways to fit the active 20th century western person's lifestyle.

Undergirding each message, however, is a gentle but firm spiritual emphasis that will support the individual in their moments of great need or in their periods of deep revelation, inspiration or internal discovery of life's awakening process.

It is hoped that each reader will find wisdom contained in these writings that strengthens, supports and stirs. If, as a result of these images, ideas and insights, your life pulse feels the quickening thrill of the Divine gently calling your spirit forward, then my task has been accomplished, indeed.

LeRoy E. Zemke
St. Petersburg, Florida

DEDICATION

From the place of profound gratitude, I dedicate this book in honor of my parents, the late Emil and Bertha Zemke.

Their practical values, spiritual strengths and unfaltering vision helped to shape my life, the hallmarks of my professional work, and thus my ministry.

In loving memory of their combined energies as parents, each individually different as father and mother, I affirm the gifting of their lives that molded and directed the course of my own life and continues to inspire me.

Contents

Contents

Thoughts for Transformation

Spiritual Insights for Positive Living

This book will enable you to experience positive, self-determining actions and results as you learn to:

* Discover keys to unlock your life purpose.
* Practice useful disciplines to gain or enhance inner clarity, spiritual insights.
* Achieve practical and useful goals.
* Accept and demonstrate prosperity.
* Change negative mental attitudes into PMA's.
* Refocus relationships.
* Heal inner woundedness.
* Open to vision and learn to live with courage, faith and a deeper sense of aliveness and love.

LeRoy E. Zemke, a native of Wausau, Wisconsin is a minister, intuitive counselor, educator and management consultant. Educated at the University of Wisconsin and Eckerd College, St. Petersburg, FL, Mr. Zemke holds a B.A. degree from University of South Florida. He was ordained in 1960 and has done advanced studies in comparative religion, transformational/depth psychology, alternative systems of healing, and metaphysical philosophy. He is internationally recognized as a leading exponent of self help, personal motivation and inner awareness principles.

His work comes from his own deepest, inner vision of what is possible for each being as they learn to express their true potential. These teachings are expressed through his ministry in one of Florida's largest West Coast New Thought Metaphysical Churches, as well as in workshops, conferences, intensives, on-going classes and in his In-Depth consultations which have taken him back and forth across the U.S. and much of Europe for over 35 years.

1

New Beginnings

"Give us wisdom to perceive Thee...intelligence to understand Thee...a heart to meditate upon Thee... and a life to proclaim Thee." **St. Benedict**
Italian founder of Benedictine Order in 530 A.D.

"One thing I do, forgetting what lies behind and straining forward to what lies ahead, I press on toward the goal." **Philippians 3:13,14**

∾

One of the greatest gifts of life is the knowledge that it is possible to renew ourselves, to begin anew, to start over again. Too often, in the face of crushing disappointment and cruel turns of a seemingly capricious fate, we face obstacles that appear and often are overwhelming. The result is that we feel blocked, restricted and very negative toward life, toward ourselves and thus toward other people.

Recently in America, as well as elsewhere in the world, we have witnessed the devastating effects of violent and freakish storms and of earth's upheavals which produced hundreds of millions of dollars of damage, to say nothing of the cost in loss of lives and human suffering. Yet out of the catastrophic and unfathomable destruction, people are putting one step after another forward to rebuild and restructure their world and their lives.

While many of us, prayerfully, may never experience such severe challenges, we must each conquer self-doubt and personal fears (loss, failure, criticism, death, ill health, poverty, et cetera), amidst a host of other challenges in order to discover the empowerment that awaits our understanding and realization.

What does it take and how does a person begin anew? What does the Truth Seeker, the New Thought student say to life when faced with obstacles or restricting attitudes?

1. **As a child of God**, each of us deserves the best that life has to offer. Therefore, we must first lay claim to the truth of our beingness. Essentially that means that regardless of the appearances about us, there is a power, an Eternal Presence that guides us, that supports us, that undergirds us. This power is available to you and me right now, where we are, regardless of what has happened in the past, regardless of how terrifying or tragic our personal circumstances may have been or may be now.

2. **We can tap**, individually, **the deepest spiritual connection or power** within us. Learn to *relax*. That means to gently let go of whatever thoughts, emotions or fears may be binding or restricting you. *Exercise*. Take a walk. Run. Do some yoga. Swim. Join a health spa and work out. Teach your physical body to reexperience a sense of well beingness. *Diet*. Eat less. Eat simply. Take in fresh foods, grains, fruit, seeds, nuts and appropriate (for you) balances of proteins, carbohydrates and starches. Learn about how your body digests its food. That way each of us can discover what our body finds agreeable and what it has difficulty with or cannot tolerate.

Give up unhealthy habits. Excesses of any kind are likely to create problems which will block one's capacity to be open, receptive and clear. We cannot easily tap our inner levels of spiritual power if we are overwhelmed with physical, biochemical burdens in our bodies.

3. **Learn to meditate** or pray consistently. Increasingly, medically and psychologically-based studies indicate that meditation when coupled with exercise, such as yoga, and dietary regimes of a simple nature (i.e., vegetarianism), produces significant changes in the outer life. Such people suffer less stress. Heart disease wanes. Hypertension fades and new evidence points to a lessening of arteriosclerosis. These are some of the benefits for our physical lives. The inner benefits are multiple and can include peace of mind, freedom from stress, more receptivity to life's movement, increased creativity, and a deeper spiritual life or connectedness to life.

Robert Schuller, pastor of the world famous Crystal Cathedral in Garden Grove, California has built his highly successful and transformational ministry upon the message that anyone and everyone can change their lives by "possibility thinking." While Rev. Schuller's message is not new to New Thought and Truth Seekers, his ministry is proof and suggests for each of us what is possible when we accept that life is for us and not against us!

New beginnings are possible for each of us whatever our circumstances or life's pattern thus far. A new relationship is possible. Or, a new attitude toward a present relationship can definitely be a "new beginning." What about a new home? Or apartment? Or a move to the city, country or village of your choice? A better job, a more rewarding work, business or profession would qualify. Improved health? Of course! A new idea or insight or creative concept is highly possible when we come from a place of seeing the best in ourselves and reach beyond present circumstances, be they images of lack or fear, loss or woundedness.

We do not, however, need to relocate to find peace of mind. We do not need to leave our jobs or professions to start over—unless, of course, such decisions have been *carefully* and *thoughtfully* weighed, considered and evaluated. It may be that we simply need to redefine the "old" or current relationship(s) in order to reach beyond the appearances of the present. In brief, we must never allow ourselves to become trapped, to become the victims of our feelings that nothing will change, that nothing can ever change. The creative choice to change our lives is always, always, *always up to us!!*

New beginnings are about having a reverence for life and permitting ourselves to stand in awe in the miracle of God's Presence in all that life is for us, individually and collectively, and all that life promises as possible. As each of us expands our consciousness to the recognition of Truth, we do come to know God as Truth. And as we come to *know* our Creator as Truth, we see our lives anew from a much higher point of view, awash with beauty, serenity, joy and peace. The possibility of our becoming stretches out before us to the edge of infinity. There is no ending. All is ever beginning.

2

Start Living Every Day of Your Life

"I have planted, Apollos watered; but God gave the increase. So then neither is he that planteth anything, neither he that watereth; but God giveth the increase. Now he that planteth and he that watereth are one: and every man shall receive his own reward according to his own labour." **1 Corinthians 3:6-8**

∾

One of the greatest restrictive beliefs in life is that there are two opposing powers, a power for good and a power contrary to good. What seems to be a contrary power (sometimes called negative or evil) is really just energy, the one and the same energy which is or has been misdirected perhaps either due to lack of understanding, limited perception or mistaken beliefs, or "improper" motivations.

The more we move toward an enlightened consciousness, the more we perceive that there is but one power, one force, ONE PRESENCE in the universe, the unlimited, unrestrictive Power of God. We struggle, however, with the world of appearances, the world of form, conditions, things, effects. We do not see the Source of Power, the I AM Presence behind all that is. The result is that we get caught, or trapped in the appearances, the illusions of reality. Perhaps we struggle with people and our narrow, often faulty views of them—not seeing them as they truly are, sons and daughters of the Living God, the Creator, Source of us all.

Others of us perhaps may suffer from delusions, false beliefs and ego-related wishes, wants and demands. These drains or pulls upon our lives detract us from our real selves, our holy or our Divine Nature.

We cannot *live* every day of our lives if we are filled with struggle, with hurt, anger or confusion about the purpose of our life. We cannot *live* every day of our lives in attempting to "Get on the good side" of the universe; i.e., "you do this for me, kiddo, and I'll do that for you!" Or, if we believe that we must fight to "overcome the enemy", then we consciously and unconsciously engage in a "battle". The result may be that in effect we "win a battle", or "overcome the enemy", but all of our systems are on alert in anticipation of the next attack!

To pursue this idea just a bit further, living from a place of limitation or fear can in no way be conceived of as its opposite: strength, acceptance, love, wholeness. Whatever it may be, individually, that keeps us from our greater self-realization, how can we turn ourselves about? How can we accomplish—*each day*—that which will give us a sense of joy, anticipation and a deep inner expectancy of our personal life? I would like to suggest some of the time-tested teachings that will help lead the way.

1. Set time aside, each day, that allows you to become still, quiet, peaceful. Even if it seems highly unlikely—given your schedule, work responsibilities, family—needs, etc.—just a few minutes spent in quieting yourself, taking a walk, listening to soothing music or allowing yourself to become still, will be useful and constructive. *"...be at peace; thereby good shall come to thee."* (Job 22:21)

2. Develop a prayer or meditation activity in your life. John Templeton, founder of the Templeton Mutual Fund Group, which now manages more than $6 billion for more than 500,000 public investors, attributes much of his success to prayer. "Give thanks to God", he says. This enables believers to rise to new heights of insight and performance. Prayer strengthens our individual sense of connection to the One Power, the One Presence. It enables and ennobles us. It allows us to know who we are beyond the illusion of form, beyond the ego, beyond appearances. It helps us to forge a link within our consciousness to the Almighty.

3. Release the old beliefs. Throw out false and restrictive ideas, as well as the outworn, the no longer useful viewpoint. These may take some time to recognize, to admit to, to be willing to let go of. Start by beginning with *forgiving others* for their mistakes, their "trespasses" whatever. Then be willing to *forgive yourself* for your own. Let go of the past. Let go slowly, gently, tenderly. Be patient with this activity. It takes persistence. It will require effort (not force) and an ongoing attitude of willingness to stay with it! Repeat the effort over and over until there is no residual of power or attachment to the outworn idea, or hurt, or misunderstanding. Until there are no rough places in your heart or consciousness for yourself or others.

4. Engage in productive activities. Attend the church, synagogue, mosque or temple of your choice. Become involved in one of those environments. *Find* a need and fill it. Find a service that you can render and perform it. It need only be one, but find it! Do it! There is nothing amiss in observing people whose skills and achievements are outstanding. But there is nothing amiss either in keeping your efforts appropriate to your interests, skills and time.

5. Live your life, one day at a time! Too many people attempt to live in the past (regret) or in the future (anxiety). Some get overinvolved with family, friends, neighbors or acquaintances. Focus on *your* life. Let others take care of their lives. That doesn't mean we should neglect our children or someone who is dependent upon our help, such as a disabled person or someone seriously ill. But it does mean that we should encourage others (who are fit and able) to attempt to take responsibility for themselves, for their lives. Do the same for yourself. Live each day, only one day at a time. Yes, plan for next week, next month, next year. But *live*—embrace, experience, enjoy—each day fully.

Living every day of our life is a *consistent daily* activity. It takes time to grow in spiritual (inner) knowledge and to realize results. The results we seek are the "pearls of great price".

Living every day is not striving, straining, pushing, demanding, begging, pleading or bargaining with God or with life. It is rather, allowing—permitting—opening—receiving—trusting and acknowledging that life is good. It is affirming that the All Knowing-Loving-Healing Power of the Universe is fully available to each of us, if we but *know* it, right where we are! We do not have to *go* anywhere to find that connection. That connection already exists from everlasting. We realize the truth of this when we can say with Bible scripture, *"Hereby we know that we dwell in him, and he in us, because he hath given us his Spirit."* (I John 4:13)

3

Discovering Your Spiritual Dimension

"Seek ye first the kingdom of God and all its righteousness and all these things shall be added unto you."
St. Matthew 6:33

"The rather earth shaking fact is that all of our abilities we develop in physical life register in, for lack of a term, or are the property of, our subtle body state."
The Bond of Power
Joseph Chilton Pearce

∾

As proposed by the two very divergent authors above, it is in the attempt and purposeful development of all aspects of our inner nature—or of all of our potential, all of our real talents, skills and capabilities—that we are truly enabled to come to know and utilize the spiritual dimension of our being. Learning about this subtle inner nature, i.e., tapping our individual potential, followed by study and organizing the information we gather, then finding useful and personally meaningful ways to put this knowledge to work in our lives often absorbs much of our lifetime. The ongoing learning process is the most creative challenge of life!

As is often cited, teachers, sages, gurus and awakened beings (so called because they not only discovered the inner way but became at one with it, i.e., they were able to embrace it fully), have set forth some significant principles as guidelines about the process. We shall examine some of these principles as practical tools that they may enable, empower and support us in this spiritually significant life discovery.

1. Study. Often discovery, of whatever nature, begins with the gathering of information. Research which has been compiled, ordered and carefully and thoughtfully presented can be useful. For example, studying the ancient sacred writings of the Holy Bible, the Vedas, the Yoga Sutras, writings of Buddha, to name a few, can be most helpful. Reading modern texts about the lives of holy men/women, their inner journeys and their discoveries can be a source of major importance.

Study also includes classes or seminars, attending church, synagogue or mosque and participating in Spiritual retreats. It may also involve formal schooling and other kinds of significant in-depth trainings and educational experiences dedicated to deepening the learning experience of the seeking individual. As we gather such knowledge, *slowly* we gain understanding and perspective.

2. Pray and/or meditate; engage in a spiritual practice. We really learn about our inner nature through the quieting of our ordinary, day to day awareness or level of mind. Prayer or meditation permits us to go beyond our mental ideas of what is true, or what we choose to believe is true about ourselves. It opens for us the doorway to God's Presence, Essence or Nature. It reveals bits and pieces of our real self, our sacred Self or divine component. It puts us in touch with our deeper yearnings. It opens (reveals) the intuitive avenue to us and paves the road for the indescribable unfolding of wisdom from which we draw revelation about our lives. Here we experience guidance: "Go ahead." "Wait." "Stop!" "Review and choose again." This revelation is possible only when we can move "outside of" or "beyond" our ordinary awareness.

3. Allow Life to teach, to direct. Let go of premature striving, efforting and willing. This is *not* to suggest that we *quit* life. Rather, it means or suggests that we *yield* the activity of pushing, manipulating and pressuring, forcing, or begging life to respond to us. It proposes that if we are in a conflicted relationship, for example, that we must stop denying our pain and choose instead to heal the hurt—in us—and allow others to do the same. If we seek a new career or job or direction, be willing first to stop, wait and listen. Listen for the still, quiet, inner prompting as a subtle urge that inclines us toward a new work or business, move or project. *Then we* *go to work!* Then we act! We get busy! We take *all* the necessary actions and steps and we make all of the efforts needed to bring it about.

4. Become involved with Life. That means that first we must become *present* and *conscious* about our own life. We must be interested in what is going on. We must take time to appreciate the little as well as the big things. It's as necessary to touch a wildflower as it is to witness the latest blast off into outer space.

We must be willing to look at the circumstances of our life. If we have pain, we need to own it, heal it and move beyond it. If we have joy or fullness or abundance, we need to claim it and allow it to really permeate our very being.

Being involved with life teaches us many important lessons. We discover the meaning of patience. We learn to honor one another in the difficult as well as the good times. We discover hidden sources of strength in ourselves, well-springs of healing reserve that bring transformation and harmony. We discover talents or capabilities we never dreamed existed. We find love where only hatred or woundedness had existed. In truth, we come to know that we are much more than what we first thought appeared to be. And we learn that regardless of how much we get to know about ourselves, we are only at the tip of the iceberg of what remains to be known.

Discovering our spiritual dimension is the most exciting internal and life changing experience we might have or anticipate. To discover means to explore, investigate, find and learn. Essentially it is an uncovering, an internal process. Yet it is also dynamic. It brings meaning to an otherwise restricted existence. It brings richness, fullness and joy where there had been only wretchedness and loss.

Our spiritual life is *not* about study, churches or places of worship, groups or disciplines. Certainly these aid the process or the journey. But in reality, our spiritual life, as we "find" our spiritual dimension, brings all of our ordinary, day to day experiences into a relationship with life that is slowly but very powerfully transforming. The experience of the death of a loved one and the grief that follows is not seen as an outrageous misfortune, but as a teacher, a compassionate thrust into parts of ourselves and of life that are bigger than we had known before. We then see another piece of the larger picture. Even savoring the fragrance of a flower we have never smelled before, opens us to unfold new vistas, new horizons, new awareness.

Let us affirm together the deep, eternal truth of our being: *"I claim my true spiritual potential in every area of my life. I confidently, lovingly and enthusiastically accept God's Unlimited Good wherever I am, in whatever I do. I reflect my talents, my gifts into all areas of my life, thus healing, nurturing and blessing all people whom my life touches."* And it is so.

4

Living in the Hand of the Divine

"I find letters from God dropped in the street, and every one of them is signed by God's name."
Walt Whitman

"The real miracle is not to walk either on water or in the air, but to walk on earth." **Nhat Hanth**

∾

The major goal of life might be stated this way: live each moment to its fullest potential. To do so means we will have no regret of past actions and no fear of the future.

To *live* life fully, however, suggests a deepening awareness of our total personal selves in such areas as health, security, family, society, world community and the many inner dimensions of our being (emotional, mental, spiritual). And to do this means that each of us must gradually come to terms with the way, the form and the process, in which we ultimately live life individually and collectively.

The way we live our life *is expressed through* our personal lifestyle as single or married householders or renters, artists or factory workers; i.e., our choices for work, business or professional expression. It includes our creative outlets, sexual preferences, our life partners or spouses, friends, our involvements with religious, cultural, social or political activities, to name but a few. The way of our life is capable of being altered when we discover a better way and other choices that are open to us. When we become open to new ways or choices, we actually access a new set or sets of possibilities with our life. Essentially, the way of our life is the avenue through which we express our uniqueness, our individuality, our worldly identity.

The form of our life involves the specific patterns we individually use to express ourselves. A pattern is a specialized frame or internal picture held in our mind; it is a set of plans we have that establishes a specific purpose or direction. The form is created, for example, by choice: "I want to get married!" Or, "I desire to go to school." We then begin to organize our thoughts, ideas, feelings and actions into an internally held image or picture as a set or grouping of plans that helps to focus our efforts. When we organize our ideas in any specific way, usually in the form of steps or plans, we are creating the pattern. If we plan to take a trip or return to school, for instance, all of the thoughts, images and concepts that are directed into specific steps are part of the pattern.

When we examine the process of our life, we actually consider the individualized activities, the *combined patterns* that create the whole. If we are building a house, we scrutinize the entire project—from inception to the idea, to the acquisition of the land, hiring an architect, then a contractor, having it built, then furnishing it and finally to moving in and getting settled. The process of our lives occurs in the day by day, moment by moment, dealing with the issues, the problems, and handling the solutions. We can call this the "nitty gritty" of our personal life involvement.

In examining the process of our lives we must make a conscious effort not to get caught in the activities or the issues of the past. Reflection, analysis and evaluation of our personal past can be very insightful and useful. Dwelling upon it excessively or compulsively indicates conflict with it which may need healing or releasing so that we can move on from it.

In a similar manner, we must not live in the uncharted future. We can think about it, plan (create) and actually move toward it. To attempt, however, to really live in the future, such as eagerly anticipating our next holiday, special event, romantic encounter or vacation period, robs us of precious focus and accomplishment in actually living in the moment. Then the now moment is never really valued. It may be perceived as boring, unimportant, non-useful and nonproductive. *And*, unfortunately, we then experience the present moment(s) of our lives as something to be endured and tolerated.

Living in the Hand of the Divine is *first,* a recognition that God, as the Ultimate Source of our life, *is* at the *center of our life*. That means many things—we are not alone, we are not alienated or separate any longer. Wherever we are, God is. *Whatever* is occurring (tragedy, illness, joy, great exhilaration), God is there, at the heart of it, as a part of it, at the very core of it. That knowledge is incredibly reassuring, affirming and clarifying. We can go forward then, with hope, faith, trust and confidence to whatever our next step might be!

Living in the Hand of the Divine is, next, a *conscious cooperation or partnership with God.* A conscious partnership with Source means we *actively* invite God into our lives. How do we accomplish this? Through prayer. Through meditation. Through becoming still (silent) and learning how to listen to the Inner Voice. It can occur as we plan our daily activities—asking God to bless our efforts and endeavors. Or, if we seek assistance in *any* area or arena of life, we must become open, receptive and allowing of God's Presence in and through our process (or pattern), our form of living. Next we must follow the inner prompting, guidance, help or nudging that may come. With God as a partner, we can move mountains—we can achieve enormous results. We can climb any mountain (or obstacle) and reach undreamed of heights. As we become consciously cooperative with God, we experience flow, instead of blockage, health instead of hurt, abundance in place of limitation, loss and lack.

Finally, as we learn to live in the Hand of the Divine, *we achieve our major goal(s)!* When we can live each moment to its fullest, we have arrived to claim one of life's most precious gifts. Life's goals vary with each of us. For some, it may be a successful career, business or completed project. For others, it may include a meaningful and deeply fulfilling relationship, or the raising of a family. For others it may involve extensive travel to foreign ports, or to man a spacecraft, walk upon the ocean floor, or found a church or school or educational institute. It may involve serving the poor, the needy, the indigent, or making the next important scientific breakthrough to cure an illness, heal the sick, or help to save the ecosystem of our planet.

In each of these areas mentioned, as well as in all possible potential goals, we experience an inner connection with Source that empowers and supports us in achieving our deepest and highest yearnings. When we live out of our potential, we experience our connection to all parts of our life and to the life we live upon the planet. Actually, we now see more clearly who we really are and recognize our unique opportunity to be upon the earth. Our potential is also spiritual awareness, our inner growth, and in the greater sense, our liberation from all that binds or restricts us. Thus we can truly move in every useful direction in our lives with confidence, consistence and commitment.

For each of us, then, to live in the Hand of the Divine implies a connecting with our life effort, our life challenges, our life circumstances. We can look at other men/women/children, races, cultures or creeds, but *we cannot* live vicariously through others. Our greatest potential cannot be developed if we are forever looking backward at the past or gazing longingly into the future. Our potential can unfold like the delicate petals of the rose, as we tend the garden, fertilize and water the plant, and allow the life force to do the rest. To have roses, we must plant roses and be responsible for their care. To have fulfillment, we must plant useful ideas, patterns and goals and tend to them, dutifully and consistently. Their flowering (maturing) is in God's Hands, even as are all things in life. Of such is the nature and the manner and the way of Living in the Hand of the Divine.

5

The Power of Love

"The Lord our God is one Lord: And thou shalt love the Lord thy God with all thy heart, and with all thy soul, and with all thy mind, and with all thy strength: this is the first commandment. And the second is like, namely this, Thou shalt love thy neighbour as thyself. There is none other commandment greater than these." **Mark 12:29-31**

∾

From popular and classical music themes, to films, novels, prose and poetry worldwide, to ancient and modern religious and spiritual teachings alike, the quality of love is extolled, sought after, praised, pined for, pursued and hoped for as perhaps no other single quality in the expression of our human nature. Confucius' definition of virtue was "Love your fellow man." Carl Rogers, the great psychologist, called it "unconditional positive regard." John the Beloved stated, "He who knows love, knows God."

Love has many faces, many unique images. Behold the look of new parents gazing into the eyes of their newborn babe, or jubilant children playing together, running, laughing and talking. Observe a pair of lovers holding hands strolling in a park oblivious to the world around them, except the world they are in. Now think of times of deep longing for companionship or being needed or wanted; think of times of deep hurt or woundedness; consider times of great pain, emotional or physical, and how much we all yearn to be free to enjoy the nurturing comfort of a friend, or the release of hurt or the soothing balm of relief from pain. That yearning to be whole again is a profound dimension of love, a region in which healing and gradual return to wholeness existThough we can carefully, critically (analytically) observe others and we can consider the many truly unlimited possibilities for love in our lives. It will not be a true probability for us until we become open, receptive to, and allowing of Love's Presence, to enter—in any form—into the heart of our lives. And how, you might well ask, is this accomplished?

1. Accept yourself, as you are, at this moment. Accepting means to embrace your flaws, flukes, fractures and follies alike without self-criticism, judgment or condemnation. Be gentle with your failures. Tell yourself, at least a dozen times a day, "I am worthy of life's best, right now, and I am open to receive it." Be content to start right where you are in life. Yesterday cannot be redone except in review. (And reviewing, reflecting and reexamining our past can be helpful.) Tomorrow ever remains a mystery—psychics, prophets, seers and wise men notwithstanding. Today is the day we have. Tomorrow is promised, but is not guaranteed. It still—always, awaits us.

2. Do what you can to heal your life! A much overused expression these days puts it in a "now" vernacular as "clean up your act"—or "get rid of your stuff," or still another phrase, "pack up your old baggage and be done with it!" They all suggest cleansing, clearing out that which blocks, hurts, wounds or stops us from being fully present in the moment. If we're over-concerned with unfinished tasks, duties, or still holding onto issues or problems of the past, we impede the flow of life or our good to us. To heal our life means to work toward wholeness and toward claiming our true nature.

3. Share yourself, your good, your talents, your knowledge, your abilities. Robert Schuller says, "Find a need and fill it; find a hurt and heal it." The nature of life is to continually flow in the direction of a vacuum. When we open up to others, we in effect, create a vacuum. As we give of our substance, our good, our talents, our abilities, we are blessed by the universe. Our true motive needs to be to love, to give, to offer something that is real, genuine and valuable of ourselves. That is the gift. We will discover in the process that, as an ancient proverb states, "He who shares a flower cannot help but wear a portion of its fragrance."

4. Dedicate your life to God and make the Source of All Life your lifetime partner! Stories abound of men and women who have made God their partner and whose lives have flourished and prospered and expressed the goodness, the fullness of good health, friends, success, prosperity, and a rich inner/spiritual life. Make God your partner by practicing prayer, often, daily if possible. And meditate, often, also daily if this appeals to you. Step away from stress! Get free of negatives in your life. Give up addictions and restricting attitudes or habits. Decide on a positive course of action in your life and really allow yourself to go all the way with it!

Love is not found in the arms of a beloved - though we might find therein a sense of connection to something larger than our limited sense of who we are. Love is not experienced in lack or pain, but through it. Life calls to us to look beyond the hurt and woundedness, to reach for the higher, greater, deeper fullness that is really, truly there. Love is discovered in the commonplace as well as in the grand and elegant. It is captured in the heart of the penitent sinner as well as the prayerful saint. It is everywhere around us, each one, in our daily lives ... in the marketplace or office, home or school. It is tapped in families, in children, adults alike. To be alive is to know love's breath. To feel warmth and caring and tenderness is to hold love's hand. To laugh and cry, sigh and die, to soar and falter, to rise and to sleep is to taste love's nectar.

We have but to listen to the multitude sounds of life, the cacophony of children talking, the thrill of great music; we have but to hold the hand of someone aged, or sick or infirm, and thus discover the bond that makes us all human.

Love is openness to life, our life, and to the ever changing pulse of it that breathes its mystical colors through the fabric of our personal tapestry. We have but to look ... and in looking but to see ... and in seeing to discover another page in our Book of Life. I wish you the power of love!

6

Transformation, The Eternal Process

Throughout the month of November, on a national and certainly on a local and community level, we are reminded of the day of Thanksgiving, appointed by Abraham Lincoln by Presidential Proclamation on October 3, 1863 to be the fourth Thursday in November. Unfortunately, it is usually only upon that one day, or perhaps at best the season or month when expressions of thanks and gratitude are vouchsafed as being appropriate.

Spiritual teachings have ever stressed the necessity for a consciousness of deep and consistent inner acknowledgment of the Greater Source of all our Good. To achieve the development, manifestation and demonstration of that consciousness, several steps are important to aid its emergence in our lives.

1. Gently, daily, acknowledge God as the Source of all that is in your life. In giving God the credit and in allowing God to be the center of your life, you begin to move away from feelings and perceptions, ideas and thoughts of lack, separation or limitation. When we truly see God as our Source, we then begin to accept the gifts, the precious gifts of our life!

2. Try gifting life in some significant manner daily. Find a person, place, or situation that you can bring your special blessing to bear upon. Bring cheer, a positive attitude in the face of a negative situation, a smile or upturned face when met by hurt, pain or frustration. Speak warmly to a stranger. Treat an animal in need with gentleness or care. Make a present of your abilities or talent—or even a tangible gift, if that seems appropriate. Let go of holding back and wondering "Should I really do this? What will 'they' think?"

3. Learn to accept, without complaint, what life gifts to you! Maybe you have a difficult relationship with a husband or wife, lover or friend, son or daughter. Allow yourself to really bless them for what they do have to offer. Give thanks for what they bring to you and look beyond what's not working at the moment! When we accept what each experience offers us, we cease resisting the hidden gift it conceals. That gift, in turn, really makes a major difference in our attitude, our personal manner, and our openness to life.

4. Be willing to risk in your gift giving! A stranger is a friend you haven't yet become acquainted with. But in order to become a friend, you must risk offering yourself. Try developing a talent or special skill beyond simply thinking about it. Risking being unsure, trekking into an unknown area of your life is absolutely necessary if growth or expansion is to occur. Your gift to yourself is your willingness to try, to move in the direction of what you seek to accomplish.

As we learn to give, we actually become more and more open to life's impulse. The broad implication for personal transformation in this process is that we really do receive from the Great Storehouse, from the deeper parts of our own being, from our Divine Self.

Another way to describe this opening to life's thrust is through our experiences, physically, emotionally, mentally and spiritually. As we become more aware of our loving attitude toward ourselves, the "problems" in others slowly disappear. As we change from being selfish and restrictive, we notice others responding to us out of love and compassion, caring and forgiving. As we change from feelings that suggest lack or limitation, we find ways for the universe to actively flow into our life to bring more good, abundance and prosperity than ever before.

Transforming our thinking is the essence or core of learning how to be open to the flow of life. When clouds mar our vision or darken our view of the spectacular landscape before us, we often suggest that God is at fault or that something, someone outside ourselves, some member of the family for instance, must change. Surely we have had nothing to do with it! As long as we continue to try to shift the responsibility and refuse to see that we generated the conditions that clouded our vision or resulted in lack, then we remain in bondage.

To become free, we must realize that God's Goodness is available to us in our journey toward our spiritual awakening. Rise free of false beliefs and attitudes and learn to clearly see and know the truth. It takes practice and daily attention to details, but soon you will attain mastery if you give yourself to the process. Be willing to accept useful change. Be willing to grow, to mature, to come into your true destined place in life. Transformation, the Eternal Process, begins now, is attained now as you relate to and identify with your inner perfection in the eternal now. All else is illusion, *maya,* transitory make believe, a puppet show against a backdrop of shadows.

7

Harvesting Our Abundance

"Give and it shall be given unto you, good measure, pressed down, shaken together and running over."
Luke 6:38

∾

In his world famous book, *In Tune With the Infinite*, Ralph Waldo Trine writes, "If you would find the highest, the fullest and the richest life that not only this world but that any world can know, then do away with the sense of separateness of your life from the life of God". Powerful and profound ideas, are they not? "Yes," you agree, "but how can I implement them?"

For centuries man has sought to understand the principle of prosperity, abundance, or the capacity to demonstrate one's good in whatever form that may take. And, for many people that idea, that principle remains elusive or, oftentimes, confusing and difficult to demonstrate. I would like to offer a few ideas for consideration that may serve as helpful keys.

1. Separation from God implies a belief in God as an anthropomorphic being that is outside of ourselves, a Supernatural Cosmic Presence that sits on a large throne in the inner circle of heaven and dispenses justice, judgment and decisions that affect each and all of us and our lives. Additionally, it implies that our lives are fixed and immutable, decreed, fated. We are locked in to a pattern and have no choices. Therefore, people with this belief perceive themselves as being inferior to or apart from this Supreme Deity. In psychology this kind of perception is called feeling like a victim. They feel powerless or have a sense of helplessness about their personal selves in relationship to their Creator. Such person's usual approach to God is in the manner of begging, pleading, cajoling, bargaining and hoping for God's attention, God's favor, God's Grace.

2. Separation from God further leads those adherents to feel, and *resultingly act,* in a manner that suggests that life is not worth living, that people are not worth the bother (especially the more difficult ones to get along with or have any kind of association with), that God is not really available to them anyway. They reason that God has really BIG PROBLEMS to deal with like mass starvation, plagues, wars and all manner of sick, troubled and dying people. Why should He be aware of or hear their personal need? And so it is that they disconnect themselves from feeling a sense of relationship with their Maker and they act in ways that tend to support their perception or belief.

3. Reconnecting with God occurs when we, as individuals, change our view or idea from God's Presence is "out there" to God's Presence is "in us". This not so subtle shift is a gradual process as we come to learn and accept that God expresses in and through and as us. Another way to say this is that each of us is an individualized unit of God Consciousness. We can actually feel God's Presence in the innermost center of our personhood, of our nature, in our heart, in and as our mind! As this shift in thinking becomes more firmly established, we become aware that the Divine Presence is, indeed, always available, always constant, always present in the moment! The next step is to make that contact a conscious union!

4. Conscious contact union occurs in such spiritual practices as prayer, meditation or yoga. In these activities, we experience a directness or sense of Eternal in the moment, the action or activity of God in our own personal being. One internal perception of this is light! Another is the sense of unconditional, universal love for all mankind. Still another level of awareness is the feeling of connectedness to all living things, to all life everywhere. As this connectedness continues to grow and expand, to deepen and strengthen, we are released from the perception of separation, of being alone, of being victimized or punished, and of helplessness. In its place, comes the feeling that our life has some purpose, meaning and direction. We begin to believe that we can be in charge of our life and set about to learn how to become all that we can be.

Then, demonstrating our good, we allow ourselves to see that abundance (prosperity) is not only available to us as a probability, but what's more, it's even a definite possibility. Abundance can now be perceived as being within our personal experience. When a person has reached a stage of internal growth where they have experienced and know that they are connected to the Source and thus are connected to all life, it also stands that everyone else is also connected to us, to each other, all others and all life everywhere! We are released from the concept that our good is or can be withheld from us by a God that is granting conditional favors. It follows, that in order to harvest our abundance, we must become open (learn how to be receptive to) life's opportunities through all of the people and all of the circumstances surrounding us. We must realize that we are not dependent upon a specific man, such as a husband or employer or whomever, or upon a specific woman, such as a wife, a mother, employer, etc., or upon a job or a certain set of conditions that have to be met to provide our good. It is a process of awakening to Ultimate Reality and transformation of our consciousness from that of limitation to our little selves into the expanded awareness of who and what we truly are as God connected beings, that we come to discover, learn and ultimately know that our good comes from the Source and that that Source (God) is ever available to us everywhere we are! Harvesting our abundance is dependent only upon how willing and receptive we are to life's unlimited flow all around us.

Dr. Donald Curtis, former minister of the Unity Church of Dallas, Texas, writes in his *40 Steps to Self Mastery*, "Think always of giving, never of getting. As you give, the receiving is automatic. Be a giver instead of a taker. Give of yourself, give of your love, give of your interest, give of your time, give of your talents, give of your treasure. Hold nothing back. Give completely. Do not bargain with God. He knows only to give Himself totally.

"As we give ourselves completely, all tensions and pressures of competitive, materialistic living disappear. Our generous giving consciousness makes it possible for us to experience that *'all things that the Father hath are mine'* (John 16:15)."

8

Claiming Our Abundance Daily

"Beloved, I wish above all things that you mayest prosper and be in health, even as thy soul prospereth."
3 John 2

∾

Abundance! The very word suggests images of that which is full, rich and unlimited. The American College Dictionary defines it as an "overflowing fullness, quantity or supply." It also means "to rise up in waves." So, it can also suggest our good coming *toward* us, much as the ocean waves keep emerging relentlessly and without cease upon the shores.

To claim our abundance implies knowing how to ask for something. Therefore, claiming suggests and invites us to make a clear and assertive, positive statement or request, wish or desire. Thus in making an effort to claim our abundance, we must learn *how* to ask for what we say we want, or request as necessary from the Source of All Life.

What follows are some significant guidelines for consideration for anyone who seeks to develop a deepening awareness and understanding of the ideas and concepts, steps and procedures that can prove useful in claiming one's abundance.

1. Divine Mind is the One and only Reality. Charles Fillmore, founder of Unity, claimed this truth 100 years ago. Today that spiritual movement has encircled the globe and this truth is taught and practiced worldwide. First, all substance, tangible and intangible, seen and unseen, is contained in the concept of Divine Mind. Therefore, all that we see in form, or all that we can think about already exists in Divine Mind or God. God is substance and may be conceived of as energy, or Spirit light, and lies back of matter and form. It is the basis of all form, yet does not enter into any form as a finality. This spiritual substance cannot be seen, touched, tasted or smelled. Yet it is more substantial than matter or physical form itself.

2. Substance is first given form in the mind! Then as it passes gradually through several stages, it becomes manifest in our lives. Here we must make our decree. *"Thou shalt decree a thing and it shall be established unto thee."* (Job 22:28). We are always decreeing, sometimes consciously, oftentimes unconsciously, and with every thought and word we are increasing or diminishing the threefold activity of substance: stillness or being centered, clarity of decree, and thankfulness for the demonstration. We cannot rush this process. Here we make our desires known to God. Flimsy-filmy-feathery ideas, halfhearted hopes or wishes, poorly defined requests, too many and confusing images, and/or unresolved inner or personal conflicts will very effectively dissipate, block, or negate the whole process. If we do not clearly know what it is we want, if we do not believe that what we ask for is possible for us to have, it isn't possible to imprint upon the invisible God Substance the good we desire to bring into manifestation. What we will perpetuate is confusion in our lives! There is an expression associated with the use of computers, "Garbage in, garbage out!"

3. Dare to give up limitation. Give up Debts. Let go of lack! In the Lord's Prayer we read and say, *"Forgive us our debts, as we also have forgiven our debtors."* Here Jesus illustrated a most significant law of mind. If we have any thought that someone has wronged us, we block the cleansing and healing power of the spirit. If we are holding onto circumstances of lack or thoughts of lack, if we accept the limitations of indebtedness, we have put bars across our mind and cannot open up to receive thoughts of healing, empowerment or inspiration. Unbar your mind and your life by forgiving yourself. Let go of the fear surrounding your debt (of whatever nature or form). Let go of worry or anxiety about finances and what you may owe anyone. This does not release you from the obligation(s), but you can part company from any thoughts that may limit you, give you no rest, make you feel inadequate or a failure. As gently and as lovingly as possible, allow any such thoughts to fall away from you. As we release (forgive ourselves), others will release and forgive us. In other words, what we do *not* hold within ourselves (in mind, in thought), we release from energizing and sending out as a lack in our lives or as images of fear to others. Once accomplished, we claim a new state of inner awareness and unerringly our good will flow toward us.

Claim then—ABUNDANCE—everywhere. Do those things which will aid and support your awareness of the Divine Source—within you. Accept new ideas and try them out. For example, if a new relationship should surface in your life and you have really been looking for such, than allow yourself the pleasure of its gifting and its discovery. Or, if you have been praying for more money and your employer or your boss should offer you additional work, accept it! Weigh the options being made available to you, but be *willing* to accept the Opportunity.

Claiming abundance is about doing our part—getting right with God—becoming still so we can *truly* know the Real Source of our great good. Once we discover for ourselves and come to that inner knowing, the *real*-ization within that there is only One Presence and One Power in the universe, we succeed in creating or demonstrating our abundant good in all things, in all ways.

I would like to end this brief discussion on abundance by quoting from Charles Fillmore's *Prosperity*:

"There is a universal law of increase. It is not confined to bank accounts but operates on every plane of manifestation. The conscious cooperation of man is necessary to the fullest results in the working of this law. You must use your talent, whatever it may be, in order to increase it. Have faith in the law. Do not reason too much but forge ahead in faith and boldness. If you let yourself think of any person or any outer condition as hindering your increase, this becomes a hindrance to you, for you have applied the law to increase it. Fear of it may cause you to become timid and bury your talent, which defeats the law. Keep your eyes on the abundant inner reality and do not let outer appearance cause you to falter."

Let there be no deterrent to your realization of the One Presence, the One Power in the universe. Let no-thing and no one limit or distract you from your at-one-ment with that Source of all good. You are now, as you read these words, the embodiment of Perfection. I invite you to claim your birthright. Claim your good (God). Claim the reality, the only Reality of your abundance each day in the forever now of your life!

9

Changes - Cycles of Opportunity

"There is a tide in the affairs of men, which, if taken at the flood, leads on to fortune; omitted, all the voyage of their life is bound in shallows and in miseries."

William Shakespeare

∾

Judith Viorst says in *Necessary Losses*, "As for our losses and gains, we have seen how often they are inextricably mixed. There is plenty we have to give up in order to grow. For we cannot deeply love anything without becoming vulnerable to loss. And we cannot become separate people, responsible people, connected people, reflective people without some losing and leaving and letting go."

Is this not a statement of the nature, the depth and the essence of change? We move inextricably toward the deepening of our lives through processes that belie description or definition. Yet our hungry intellect reaches for morsel after morsel of understanding regarding the dynamics of change regardless of its inconsistent and even difficult nature.

To grow, in nearly every area or avenue of life, is to change from one form to another. A seed is planted and literally thousands of microscopic and minuscule cellular changes bring about the development and ultimate maturation of a full grown plant ... a radish, a rose, or a redwood.

A human child is conceived and a miracle begins. So many changes occur around the conception and development of an embryo from the earliest moment of fusion of sperm and egg (fertilization) that whole systems of sciences have unfolded to help us *begin* to appreciate the wonder, the "Cosmic Technology" involved as they attempt to explain our biological and genetic origins.

Further changes occur as we are born and start our human journey ... changes which are noted, connoted and denoted by scientists and sociologists, doctors and dentists, mothers and fathers, teachers and trainers, psychics and psychologists, and saints and sages the world over. Try as we might, we cannot know them all let alone try to catalogue or categorize or define them.

How, then, can we make wise uses of so many changes on our spiritually awakening journey of life? How can changes of our physical aspects, our emotional, psychological and mental components be perceived as opportune? And, even more so, the deeper, inner world of internal changes so often addressed in the transformational process? I would suggest:

1. Be open to life. Life's impulse is to grow, awaken, deepen. The universe is forever pouring itself into manifestation. Therefore, allowing ourselves to be conscious, imaginative, intuitive and willing to be receptive to what life brings our way allows us to receive the gift(s) our encounters and involvements bring us. Resistance tends to block or curb us. As human beings, we have the capacity of choice which enables us to know more of our capabilities or assets, our options or possibilities beyond our perceptions, beyond our tendency to measure, capture and control life.

2. Live responsibly. Learn to take control of random thoughts, dark moods or difficult circumstances or situations by *courageously* facing them, endeavoring to move beyond any emotional charges and thereby discern possible positive solutions. Then direct all efforts to move in the direction of the deliberated decisions and follow through with positive appropriate behavior. It is unwise and truly unproductive to dedicate ourselves to resolving other people's conflicts while neglecting our own. In the larger picture, we cannot heal other people or fix their lives. We can heal our own lives and thereby be a model for those with whom we live and move and share our lives.

3. Surrender to Life. Let us examine our life in the light of those who have awakened such as Jesus, Buddha, and many others. To surrender to life means to yield, to stop trying to change others to our viewpoints, our favorite beliefs or attitudes about right and wrong, life and death, health and wholeness, or whatever. We each have our own connection to Source and can discover it for ourselves if we can get past our ego needs, attachments, or our personal need to be right. Surrender involves giving up struggle, attitudes of loss, being a victim, and allowing life to truly enlighten us. Real surrender is about yielding our personal will to God's Will, or as Roy Eugene Davis puts it, "...to serve the cause of evolution."

4. Live with vision. One of the significant reasons for human suffering, lack of fulfillment and personal frustration is that, too often, we are over-concerned about what we want or think we want and are not significantly concerned about what life wants of us. When all or most of what we seek reflects the attitude, "What's in it for me?", we cannot truly live from a place of inspired vision or noble or altruistic intention. To live with vision means that we must make conscious choices to do three things.

"First, if there is anything that we need to change, it has to be acknowledged and a *decision* made to do what we can to assist ourselves in the direction of fulfillment. Two, a *commitment* must be made, so that we take a stand and are determined to follow through with appropriate actions. Three, we have to *know how to proceed and then do so*, without looking back and without being afraid. This is it - the vision of possibilities and decision to rise to the occasion, firm determination and high resolve, and then living according to the highest and best ways we know." (Roy Eugene Davis, *How to Have the Courage to Live and to Prosper*)

To see changes then as opportunities awaiting our involvement, our commitment and our hidden talents requires a shift; sometimes a small, almost inconsequential effort will do; othertimes a major overcoming, yielding, releasing and efforting seems necessary—all to the point that we cannot grow to be more or awaken to our true spiritual nature unless we are ready to embrace the unlimited possibilities that beckon us—ever calling us to discover more of our real nature, our sacred self, our forever link with our Divine Source!

10

The Vision of Becoming

"After a person has attained the highest perfection while in the body, he can attain the Supreme Vision. With pure understanding and controlled thoughts and actions, keeping his own counsel, being moderate in all things and practicing deep meditation, removing from his consciousness everything that is not God-like, such a person becomes purified and knows Ultimate Truth."

Bhagavad Gita

∾

Life imbues each of us with deep, powerful urges, urges to express the Creative Principle in any of a variety of activities such as writing, musical composition, singing, painting, sculpturing, to name but a few. Sometimes these urges, these inner promptings are to learn about herbs, plants and minerals and develop a compassion and sensitivity for their use in the art and skill of healing. For others these urges are subtle "callings" to study and explore physics, or chemistry, electricity or sound, leading them to become physicists or chemists, engineers or technicians. It is essentially the same Creative Energy that leads one to become a musician, or poet, or dancer, and another an architect, or doctor, or lawyer, et cetera. For some, these inner urges incline or impel them to probe the mysteries of the universe through scientific research. Still others are led to seek, to discover their ancient roots through study and scholarship into antiquities, customs and cultures. In all instances, the urge to learn, to probe, to discover something about and of ourselves is an expression of our yearning to discern the true nature of who we are.

Our vision of becoming is really about honoring, at the deepest level of our being, the capacity to tap the ineffable

- our most profound image, picture or sense of who we are and what God is. This vision is born with us. It arises beyond the circumstances of our birth, our parents, relatives, family or social conditions. It emerges through limitations, it stretches beyond creeds, color or conventional wisdom. It calls to us in times of tribulation or trauma or trial. It speaks to us in powerful and awesome moments of inspiration. It beckons to us in the presence of greatness and meekness alike. It seems to encourage us in our times of heaviest stress or incapacity. The ineffable image is always there, always just under the surface of our consciousness. Most often we are able to sense it or feel it when we are still, quiet, undisturbed by the surface winds that blow across the plains of our lives.

To capture the vision that is individually ours, some steps to secure, attune to the essence or perception of it are necessary. The following ideas and practices can be useful in allowing, aiding and supporting your vision to surface.

1. Become still. As often as possible, let there be some special selected time to gently quiet the conscious mind. Stop thinking about people! Stop focusing on a problem situation, your own or that of someone else. Stop rushing about to accomplish anything. Become still. Settle down.... Relax.... Just be.

2. Release, release, release! Be here now. The past is over, done with. We cannot really accomplish anything by attempting to redo it, to restructure it, to change or reshape it mentally, emotionally or even physically. Give up the past. Cease trying to control other people who are part of the past or even a part of your present. Allow them to be themselves. Stop grieving over or musing about the past. If in the present you need to put a particular situation in order or to rest, if you need to complete a task, perform a duty, or forgive a person, do it! Then, let it be. Move on. Releasing allows us to become aware of and sensitive to our inner being, our deeper vision or purpose and not be trapped by the outer appearances and conditions of our lives.

3. Pray without ceasing. From the Bible to the Koran, from the Bhagavad Gita to the philosophy of the Sufi, prayer is invited and encouraged. Although it has many forms, prayer is a process that enables the practitioner to enter a deeper, inner, reflective and receptive state. This state or level of consciousness permits or empowers the individual to recognize a personal connection to the ineffable, the Source of ALL LIFE. And it is at this moment of connection that one may gain knowledge or a perception of one's inner vision, or perchance some understanding about his or her sacred self.

Prayer, in reality, as is also true of meditation, allows us to stop focusing upon the outer appearances in life. It permits us to *discover* our personal revelation, our personal vision, our personal understanding in a more precise manner. It frees us to learn what is necessary to enable us to not only "listen" more exactly to our inner promptings, but to identify them accurately and learn how to become attuned or sensitive to our real nature. We continuously discover that our life is actually an enormous opportunity of awakening, growing and learning. We benefit, we progress on all levels of our being and we incorporate and apply what we discover to our personal circumstances.

4. Live your life! As obvious as that statement appears, may of us do not know how to honor our own life. We live vicariously through our family, children, parents, spouse or friends. We select heroes/heroines whose lifestyles speak to us. Some people are addictive and compulsions rule them such as sex, food, alcohol or drugs, nicotine, et cetera. All of these will either restrict or shut off one's vision. In such forms of living, a person's inner nature can only break through in trauma or pain, or in occasional revelations such as in dreams, in encounters with spiritually awakened individuals, or perhaps in "spontaneous" situations wherein life reveals clarity.

Living your life implies a stepping free of boundaries, self-imposed or otherwise, that will permit your deepest yearnings to emerge. Be willing to handle or embrace your own personal experiences. Give permission to yourself to make your own discoveries about your life. If you seek to be an astronaut, a farmer, or a stock broker, pay attention to what images, yearnings, inclinations or motivations surface from within you. Then *act* upon them. Move in the direction of their accomplishment, their actual manifestation.

Whatever you dare to dream, to vision, or discover, if you are rightly resolved, begin today to move in the direction of fulfillment. The power of the universe is behind (and within) you when you are moving in harmony with life's purpose. No person and no external forces can prevent you from achieving your rightful goals and experiencing your destined fulfillment when you are in tune with the One Power, the Power of God. Be open to this Power. All that remains is to do your part.

"Courage then to claim it; that is all! But courage you have; and the knowledge that we are pilgrims together wending through unknown country, home." (Fra Giovanni)

11

Embracing the Power of Forgiveness

"If you are serious about the sufferings of mankind, you must perfect the only source of help you have — yourself." **Jerome Frank**

∾

When we consider the term "release", or the word "forgiveness", many images, thoughts and feelings may emerge that can cause us to feel a sense of frustration or inadequacy. Perhaps we know from past experience that the act of trying to release a habit, an outworn idea or an old attitude, a past mistake, a broken relationship, or perhaps a problematic issue in our home, our business or work, or even in our approach to our spiritual life may bring only anxiety or more disappointment. The efforts we make to forgive and release may be helpful, but somehow the situation or circumstance may still remain resolutely fixed in our life.

Fear, thoughts of failure, or constant remembrances of old hurts often serve as blocking patterns that stop the action of forgiveness or release. Some of the reasons we hold onto these patterns may be: (a) God cannot reveal the change we seek because we're not "good enough", (b) we really need to suffer (which comes from guilt), or (c) that something larger than ourselves is to blame and consequently our good health, our good relationship, our appropriate job or contentment and inner peace is consistently delayed, blocked or unavailable.

As we awaken upon the spiritual path, we discover that the action of release begins in our consciousness, from the deep innermost part of our Divine Self. The guidance (inspiration) from our Innate Spirit gradually emerges into our thinking and feeling and finally into our personality world.

This emerging action of release is signaled by a strong, powerful desire to refocus the old idea, or reframe the limited image or perception. When that happens, a positive change in direction and understanding occurs, resulting in a new and fulfilling change in our experiences.

To begin the work or process of release or forgiveness, here are a few suggestions that will aid a different perspective to emerge, or a new way to "unblock" and acknowledge the changes and directions you may wish to manifest in your life.

1. Daily affirm slowly, in an accepting and gently caring way, "I am free. I am releasing and blessing this experience (name it) in my life at this time! I give it to God. I accept God's love for me, now. So be it." Affirmations are powerful, positive, life supporting self talk statements!

2. Allow whatever conflicting feelings, attitudes or emotions as may surface to do so in a manner that will help you to let them go. Talk them out (with someone you trust) or verbalize these ideas aloud in the quietness of your personal space (apartment, home, car, garden, etc.). Or, if you prefer, write out your feelings and ideas and any conflicts in a journal or on sheets of paper. Either talking or writing is a form of release and will help to allow inner freedom to begin to emerge. Be willing to be persistent with this exercise. It may take some time to work, effectively. But, if pursued, it will offer you some positive results. Try not to personalize your feelings or thoughts; just permit them to flow. Be non-judgmental, critical or evaluative of your thoughts at this time. At the end of seven days (just one week), you will see some positive results. Then keep up the work.

3. Permit yourself to now **affirm**, in a new way, **the new energy** you are now opening yourself up to experience. Your real, larger nature is already waiting to express itself. You have but to know it, to claim it, to accept the realization that as Roy Eugene Davis says, "God is expressing as me, as the ocean expresses the wave". An affirmation to acknowledge this new sense of your Real Self might be: "*I know, I express, I am experiencing the Presence of Love and Healing in all areas of my mind, body and being. I accept my Unlim-*

ited Good, my deep inner peace, and God's Loving Presence. I give thanks."

4. Enter into a prayerful or meditative state following the above suggestions. Meditation, for example, when practiced simply and clearly, allows one to tap the Inner Presence, the Transcendent Self. Thus, in allowing oneself to touch, tap or feel into this Larger Reality, there is a profound shifting of energy. As the deeper components of our being emerge, into a more conscious relationship with our ordinary states of awareness, we experience healing, integration and a sense of purposefulness about ourselves, our lives and our painful past. We can, in effect, let go of issues, problems, painful woundings and begin to live from a place of empowerment.

Embracing or allowing the power of forgiveness, then, is in reality a major opportunity to remind ourselves that God is ever-present and *always* ready to sustain, to nurture, to love, to strengthen, to bless us and to heal us. The Power of God is forever and always the One Power, the One Reality from which we came and into which we unfold. In trusting this, we become more at peace with ourselves. We lose the need to control. We yield our concerns. We seek to honor our life and our experiences. We surrender to God and allow God to be "in charge." We live out of that place that permits us to know that life—the rich, unlimited power of the Source, is truly ours for the asking. And, we are invited to partake of this power—this gift—as we let go and release, the issues of fear, loss and conflict dissolve.

12

Awakening to Our Higher Consciousness

"What? Know ye not that your body is the temple of the Holy Ghost which is in you, which ye have of God and ye are not your own?" **1 Corinthians 6:19**

∾

Most spiritual traditions, both modern and ancient, suggest in their teachings that mankind can awaken (become more aware) and directly experience "higher" consciousness. What varies from one tradition to another are the methods, the various approaches to how this awakening should appropriately occur. For example: practitioners of yoga, Zen Buddhism, Hinduism, as well as Christian mysticism, Christian prayer, New Thought philosophies, Christian Science, etc., etc., each espouse specific disciplines as being necessary and preparatory for one to awaken to higher awareness, or to one's essential Divine Nature.

It would appear from all the emphasis placed upon techniques, methods and systems, that practicing the "right" one guarantees or secures the awakening experience.

For example, meditation. Now widely taught throughout the east and west as *a way* to access our inner nature, meditation has many variations of specific forms or formulas. Each form is said to help bring about the desired objective of contacting some deep, inner level or some greater or "higher" dimension of consciousness. Yet, in spite of the proliferation of approaches, of forms or formulas to make this inner contact, the experience of such contact, ultimately, remains beyond intellectual understanding alone or the "guarantee" of one method in favor of another.

What must become absolutely clear to the neophyte as well as the most advanced student is that the *process* of the method(s) helps to create the appropriate physical, emotional, mental and spiritual environments for the inner awakening experience. The process, or approach, or tradition is merely the "staging" necessary for the "action of the play" (or the activity of our consciousness) to occur.

"Yoga", for example, as described by Dr. Rammurti Mishra in his book, *The Fundamentals of Yoga*, (Harmony Books, New York), "is mastery of mind. It is a *process* of dehypnotism. Yoga presents a scientific way and methodical effort to attain perfection through the control of the elements of the physical, metaphysical and psychical natures."

We might surmise from these statements that yoga is a lot more than the stylized image of a slim yogic devotee, Indian or otherwise, who has occult powers and bizarre behavior. And yoga is much more than a system of exercises for people who wish to learn to relax, gain freedom from stress or lose weight.

Yoga helps to create an *inner* and an outer environment that gradually strengthens our capacity to be receptive and open to our higher or more subtle nature.

The same might be said for other disciplines such as meditation, contemplation, prayer, Tai Chi Chuan, to name only a few. The process, may include as important elements for stirring the awakening such considerations as breath control exercises, relaxation techniques (simple or complex), the use of images or pictures, sounds (chanting of mantras), or a variety of physical activities. These steps might be compared to the rungs of a ladder. The rungs are steps in the process of climbing to the next level or plateau. Each rung (step) is helpful, necessary and useful. The ladder is a tool (of however many needed rungs or steps), but it is not the only tool that will aid the activity of climbing. Once a goal, level or plateau has been attained, the tool is set aside.

Awakening, or becoming more conscious about our deeper inner nature, is not about finding the "right" method or key or system or discipline. Many sincere and genuinely interested students become trapped in defending the rigors and benefits or denying the positive and helpful merits of one method over another, or one process above or lessor than another. True awakening utilizes many keys. Finding an appropriate discipline (process) that is best for an individual is a matter of individual sensitivity, receptivity and internal resonance to the inherent truth or validity of the discipline at hand.

To facilitate your awakening journey, several suggestions are offered for consideration.

1. Begin a specific discipline (or training) on a specific day of the week at a specific time of the day. This act helps to create order in your approach to and your development of a relationship with your Inner Nature. Decide on *prayer* or *yoga* or *meditation*. Do not try to do one discipline one day then switch to another discipline the following day. To do so, one week later you will not only be confused, but you will have discovered no real benefit.

2. Be cautious of systems or methodologies that promise "instantaneous transformation" and/or "great, giant quantum leaps" in a workshop, in a class, over a weekend, by the end of the month, as a result of some "magical" act, or touch, or expected benefit from being in a "holy place", in a "charged environment", or the like. While any of the above can be, and sometimes are helpful to sincere students—depending upon a brief, one time encounter with a teacher or facilitator of some mental/emotional/psychological process is illusory. It feeds the ego of the student who wants to believe in "fairy dust", the something for nothing, pie in the sky attitude which is common to many people who are not grounded, whether or not seekers of Higher Awareness, Inner Awareness or Higher Consciousness.

3. Finally, be truly willing to learn honestly, slowly, painstakingly about yourself. Be willing to change patterns of your behavior or life style that are no longer beneficial or useful. If professional help is needed to overcome a habit or an uncompromising attitude or behavior, seek out a qualified, certified professional counselor or therapist whose life reflects a profound commitment to the sacred, or to the Life Principle. Be open to inner growth and its subtleties ... slowly. Affirm the miraculous in your life and allow yourself to adjust, as necessary, to the inner direction, the intuitive impulse that will slowly, clearly and without fanfare unfold within the context of your life. Consummate insights will begin to emerge. Deep, clear inspirations will surface bringing healing release, inner freedom and understanding.

Expect a miracle! Expect the miracle of awakening to your higher consciousness. Awakening is, ultimately, an emerging, a revelation of one's deeper, true, Inner, Sacred Self, freed from the clatter and clutter of wishes, wants and the debris of living life focused on worldly expectations. We awaken to thus know ourselves, not to remain chained and bound by someone else's idea of us. This then is perhaps the real message underlying Shakespeare's famous passage in Hamlet, "This above all - to thine own self be true; and it must follow as the night the day, thou canst not then be false to any man."

13

Love - the Heart of Our Divine Connection

"Start the day with love, live the day with love, end the day with love." **Sri Satya Sai Baba**

∾

Of the vast kaleidoscope of human emotions and yearnings, perhaps love alone conjures up and evokes more subtle images, more deeply stirs our hearts, more brilliantly fires the imaginations, more urgently quickens the pulses, and more exuberantly lifts the Spirit! From time immemorial, people have tried to capture its essence in prose and poetry, in dance and drama, in art and sculpture, and in music and song. Love is sought for by young and old alike, pursued equally by the high and mighty alongside those of simple estate, the humble, the lowly. Love is hungered for by rich and poor alike, scientist and savant, saint and sinner. People search for love and try to bargain for it. We hope, dream and pray for it. Our spirits beg and plead for love. We aspire to know it from the deepest reaches of our being. What is this thing called love?

Often, when we look at the world and are endlessly reminded of pain, tragedy and trauma, it is profoundly difficult to see any manifestation of love or even to allow ourselves to "practice the Presence of God" by looking upward, reaching for hope, expecting a miracle, or simply trying to do our best in whatever way or form that may be.

With all of our deepest yearnings to attempt to capture and experience love, it is singularly important to *allow* the dimensions of Spiritual Love to become known to us within the context of our lives. This can be accomplished as we, on an individual basis, examine and explore our lives to invite and embrace a more "tangible" demonstration of the love experience.

(a) Daily, begin to turn from limiting fears and feelings to positive and supportive perceptions and reactions about life. Our choices are ways to direct our energies to allow the inner dimensions of our divine nature to emerge. Choose to express kindness, gentleness, humility and forgiveness instead of hurt, anger, harshness or brashness. When you do so, note how this causes a shift in your feelings, in your receptivity and openness.

(b) Decide to take action toward positive changes in your life. Studies of successful people in all walks of life consistently reveal that success follows when people make positive choices about changes. Change is defined as "movement toward, making different". It suggests making a material (physical), emotional, mental/psychological difference so that the thing or condition is noticeably other than it was.

A decision releases energy. It permits a new insight, an intuitive awareness, an emotional freedom to emerge. As this is supported in each area of life, slowly those issues that block or deny our freedom, our sense of who we are, slip away. We don't have to "fix the problem" as such. We need to focus on the solution. For example, if we have a digestive disorder, taking medication or seeking professional help is a possible solution. Yet, perhaps focusing on how to live in a healthy manner in all ways is the larger and more significant goal and solution.

(c) Resolve to live every day fully. So much of life is put "on hold", to delay our good to the future. We anticipate birthdays, anniversaries, special events and occasions and make plans accordingly. What about experiences of the moment, day-to-day? If it's raining, put on a raincoat and get on with the job at hand. If a diet needs to be started, begin now! Find out what needs to be done, research what must be researched —and start. If the goal is meditation or starting a new job, healing a relationship or finding a new apartment, today is the day to begin! Today is the beginning of the rest of your life!

Loving, then, is about living life. It is not only about the special, hoped-for, dreamed-of relationship with a companion. It is the expression of all of our yearnings in useful, creative and fulfilling ways. Loving is not a sexual act to be hotly pursued or pined for, but rather a yielding to life's greatest impulses—to feel the kiss of sunlight through misty foggy places! Our Divine Connection is encouraged through our conscious cooperation with the world around and within us. If we are surrounded with music and yet only see the struggle it may have taken to birth the symphony, we lose the gift the music can bring us. If we are surrounded by needy people, begging and pleading for attention, it is only when we can move beyond their pressing and passionate pleas for help that we can hear their spirit sing or feel the exuberant release of their joy.

Brother Lawrence, a 17th century mystic who is honored today as a spiritual inspiration, practiced love through humility of service. He knew the meaning of pain. He was wounded and lame after a stormy life as a soldier. He had to work through much anxiety and remorse. He achieved his mastery through serving his brother monks in the bustle of a huge monastic kitchen, cooking for the whole order. Regular periods in the chapel spent in prayer and meditation led him to "practice the Presence" continuously, in the kitchen as well as in the chapel.

Love is about allowing all of the aspects of our varied lives, the tender and the tumultuous. Then the sacred and the profane become a chalice of our lives. It is only when we can clasp the vision of all that we dare to dream and forge that vision into the fabric of our daily lives that our Divine Connection is made real.

"I know, that, for the right practice of it, the heart must be empty of all else; because God wills to possess the heart alone; and as He cannot possess it alone unless it is empty of all else, so He cannot work in it what He would unless it be left vacant for Him." (Brother Lawrence)

14

Creating A New Reality

"Ask and it will be given unto you; seek and you will find; knock and it will be opened unto you."
Matthew 7:7

∾

How often have we said to ourselves, "If I could just have another chance to try again, I'd do it differently next time"? Or perhaps, "What I would give to have another opportunity to do better in my job" or "to change the way I behave toward my spouse, family or friend." What we may know but sometimes forget is that the opportunity for beginning anew or starting in a different direction is already our privilege, our very special gift from the Source of all life!

Ancient spiritual teachings as well as New Thought writers tell us repeatedly that every single moment is alive with the very substance or essence of the Spirit of God. And, it is this very essence, or vital life force that interpenetrates, undergirds and sustains life that is available to us wherever we are, whatever we are doing, whatever may be occurring (positively or negatively) in our life.

There is a creative principle or law that is ever available to us when approached rightly and wisely. At the very moment man is able to contact and realize the law, he will at once experience the benefits of growth, power and understanding. It is the realization or direct experience of the law in action that determines manifestation.

For example, an electrician does not pray and then just wait for the electric energy to decide to serve him. No, he studies, practices and gains knowledge of the laws of conduction and transmission of energy in order to learn how to *consciously* and with clear intent cooperate with the principle that governs electrical energy. Once he learns or gains this information, he sets up appropriate and proper machinery which provides the means to generate and direct the power. Once he understands the principle, he can snap a switch and operate giant machines, computers, create heat, flood a city with light and set forth into motion countless other devices which are powered by this form of energy. He can repeat this principle as often as he chooses, as long as he does not disturb the mechanics or violate the law governing the use of the energy. The operation of all scientific laws is thus the same, including the science of our being!

To create means or suggests a process whereby something, often new, is brought into being. The creative person possesses a power, sometimes known to us as imagination, which has a potency and brings about a state of actual expansion or manifestation!

Kenneth Thruston Hurst writing in *Spiritual Insights for Daily Living* (published by S.F.F., Independence, Missouri), suggests that "this building block of spirit and matter alike is the very source which creates what we perceive outside ourselves and generates all that is within. We draw this energy into our thought processes, and with its help, *we create* what we want...for our lives!"

The teaching is not new. Jesus taught us that we must ask (cooperate with universal law or principle) and what we seek shall be granted or given. That means that we have choice to receive our good...it is not being withheld from us; it is not being denied because of some karma or bad influences, evil forces or unslain dragon.

Raymond Holliwell writes in *Working With the Law*, "There is a marvelous inner world that exists within man, and the revelation of such a world enables man to do, to attain and to achieve anything he desires within the bounds or limits of Nature." Remember William Shakespeare's famous words, "The fault, dear Brutus, is not in our stars, but in ourselves, that we are underlings."

Creating a new reality is not only possible, it is our right. As children of God we must remember the promise of Luke 1:37, "*For with God, all things are possible*." Remembering this takes effort, patience and practice. Daily efforts such as releasing our past mistakes (or misdeeds), forgiving ourselves and thus others, and affirming our contact with our Inner Wisdom through meditation, prayer, or other significant spiritual practices brings about the changes we seek.

It is in *ask*ing that we begin to be open, to search, to discover and, if we are receptive, we *do receive*. It is in *seek*ing, learning, practicing and applying what we have discovered, discerned and digested that we truly do *find*. And it is in *knock*ing, or continuously affirming our Inner Truth or Wisdom in each area, issue or avenue of our life's experiences that the secret of life and all its mysteries shall be *opened* unto us!

15

Life, The Positive Creation

"To get to the core of God, at His greatest, one must first get into the core of himself at least, for no one can know God who has not first known himself. Go to the depths of the soul, the secret place of the Most High, to the roots of the heights; for all that God can do is focused there." **Meister Eckhart**

∾

Life is composed of a series of choices. Some choices are easily discovered, nonthreatening and without conflict. Others emerge only after severe reflection, painful deliberation or long and often exhaustive considerations for extended periods of time. What choices do for us is to allow or permit us to discover and access the emerging boundaries or perimeters of our deepest nature, our soul's essence.

Choices really define parts or aspects of our experience by allowing us to see the result of our actions or our deeds, such as when we overeat or overindulge in drink, or when we work too hard or too intensely. Such experiences teach us that overindulgence or overwork creates problems or imbalances, not only in our physical bodies, but in our day to day lives on our physical, emotional and psychological well-being also.

In the physical world such as in the market place, we have records, meticulously kept, that allow us the opportunity to study the actions (choices) of others as well as perhaps of our own creation. When we invest money, buy and sell property, enter into relationships, take a job or choose a career, the results of choices can be seen, appreciated and understood with varying levels of awareness and sophistication through books, our past education, through classes, and through many forms of information as well as our own past experience. This enables us to more wisely approach our lives and new challenges and opportunities with clarity and precision, with clearer vision and a deeper sense of the ranges of possibilities open to us.

When we make choices, however, that have more to do with our inner nature, such as what we will study to improve our mental and/or spiritual life, or what we will surround ourselves with in creating an acceptable and inspiring environment, we tend to choose those books, or select those experiences, or things that require a deeper level of awareness or greater degree of perception than our secular life prepares us for.

Here we are choosing out of a sense that we are dealing with the unknown, or hitherto unexplored dimensions of ourselves. This kind of choice is often uncertain and very difficult. We make many efforts, sometimes a significant number of false starts. At this level of our life, the carefully detailed reports of our business activities, or perhaps the specificity of our doctors' intricate medical analysis cannot really serve us. When we deal with our own personal inner life, we enter a region that is unfamiliar both in context and content, even though others have entered and experienced that region within themselves before us. Our own experience is beyond comparison to what others have encountered and left some written record of. We are entering our own domain, something uniquely our own. It is at once thrilling, exhilarating, frightening and confusing. Yet we are urged, nudged and drawn forward to the inner journey.

Enlightened teachers and holy people for thousands of years have left writings such as are contained in the Bible, the Bhagavad Gita, the Vedas, and other sacred texts that speak about high level wisdom and revelation that is ours when we choose to "think on these things" (Paul to the Philippians). We are encouraged to study, meditate, reflect and pray on a daily basis and utilize the content, the inspired words and ideas, concepts and images of the writings and slowly integrate, permit them into our life. This choice affects our spiritual and inner life in ways that are enormously profound. Out of this choice emerges an incredible depth and clarity (wisdom) about ourselves that permits each of us to begin "to get to the core of God."

Currently, much is being made of the effective use of time management. We are encouraged to prioritize our chores and duties in order to accomplish specific goals or plans. For those who have attempted this, the positive benefits are well known. But what of the time that is wasted, lost, frittered away or simply idly spent? How does the choosing of where we place or focus our energy affect the quality of our lives?

In the awakening process, it is our resistance to the inner movement of Spirit by our old choices, our preconditioned responses, false notions or ideas, problematic attitudes, etc. that creates and recreates the difficulties that we encounter. The challenge is to choose to let go, give up or release, or to choose to continue to justify, intensify and give even more importance to our limitations, weaknesses or lack!

If life is a positive creation and if we choose to see it that way, then each experience can be seen to have meaning and value; every experience can teach us and inspire us. Certainly, at times, there will be seemingly inexplicable hurt, anger, pain, fear and loss. But out of it will emerge strength, clarity, vision and new understanding of ourselves that take us "to the depths of the soul, the secret place of the Most High, to the roots of the heights; for all that God can do (be) is focused there."

Perhaps in our choices we need to be guided more by the call of the Inner Voice, The Spirit of God, and less by our human wishes, wants, needs and compulsions. Perhaps we shall attain to purity only when we stop searching for it outside ourselves. When we stop searching for it in others, we cease struggling with their imperfections. In other words, we stop attempting to make them be perfect in ways we are not!

It is when we finally accept the incredible innate beauty of our own being that we have made one of life's most significant choices! That choice then leads us to transformation, to our awakening and to the ultimate realization that we carry the seed, the germinal essence of our divinity at the core of our being. That indwelling divinity is already urging us onward, yearning to be expressed within the majestic framework and unparalleled beauty of our own personal tapestry! It is here that life is a positive creation! It is here that we finally choose to make of our life the sacred, holy gift. It is here that we accept Life for all that It offers to us!

16

Radiance, The Light Within

Everywhere in the ancient teachings, the Bible, as well as the enlightenment traditions and especially in New Thought and the broad metaphysical field itself, the statement is made over and over in myriad forms and ways, *we are unique expressions of pure consciousness.* We work through mind and body to participate in the unfolding drama of our earthly life! This truth has some powerful insights for us as we consider certain ways to examine its broader implications and applications for our unfolding daily life.

To be a unique expression of the Divine signifies that each of us, or each soul has capacities, talents, special knowledge and perhaps, as yet, unrefined skills that are particularly our own. These potentialities or (as yet) unmanifest abilities are our real birthright, our true personal inheritance, our very own gift from God. Whenever we acknowledge our connection to the Source and give or allow ourselves permission to utilize or develop these gifts, we begin to awaken to the Radiance, the Light Within. We awaken or become more conscious when we become aware that we choose to really focus on our essential beingness or upon developing our actual talents or skills or special abilities and take those steps that are necessary for them to emerge in and as the fabric of our lives.

We are taught that the more pure and refined the physical body, the subtle essence of the body, and the mind - the more easily can soul influences express as intended. This suggests that there is the likelihood of little success on the spiritual path without intentional discipline motivated to insure that the body is clear and responsive to the imprint from the soul.

How is this cleansing accomplished?

(a) Rest, recreation, positive nutrition and suitable exercise most certainly apply at the physical level.

(b) On the emotional level, restricting, blocking and painful issues are cleared as a result of releasing, letting go of one's attachments to ego-centered demands or needs. This can be achieved by personal effort and/or by the help of appropriately trained facilitators, therapists, or other qualified persons or spiritual teachers. The practice of patience in the face of all circumstances will be useful in all approaches to clear emotional demands or issues.

(c) The mental field or level is cleansed as a result of superconscious forces which become available to us as we take responsibility for ourselves by or through the practice of prayer, meditating correctly, and in a larger, more general sense, by becoming open to our infinite good through all of the above.

(d) Additionally, we become receptive to our greater good through study of the ancient and modern teachings, sacred and inspired writings, and by developing an underlying trust in God in all matters. Disciplines which are useful as contributing to the ordering and renewing of the body, nervous system and mental field are most helpful also.

Once we have consciously and consistently made efforts to become much more open to our uniqueness in all areas of our life, our life becomes a statement of God's Perfect Will. We achieve this state as we stop thinking and speaking about our troubles, our limitation, our problems or the confusions of others. We focus instead upon what we have discovered to be the true and real nature of our being.

Roy Eugene Davis writes in *Truth Journal,* "We all, every one of us, deserve the best that life has to offer. We also have a duty to live up to our highest potential". Some will say, "the flesh is weak" or "it's only human to err". Remember, the soul, the real being is not weak, it is not helpless or frail. God, manifesting in and through and as us is the divine nature each of us is connected to. When we remember that truth, then we can affirm that our real choice is to move in the direction of staying open (receptive) to all that our life, our soul, our being has to offer us!

The Light Within each of us is triggered by our inner/outer choices. Is it our choice to concentrate upon what isn't working in ourselves? In others? In life? Or, do we recognize that it is our divine opportunity to begin from where we are, with all of the useful skills and tools of our life available to us? We can choose to first make a real difference in our own life, then with our husband or wife, with families, partners, and then in more extended fashion, within the world we live in.

Our Light Within then is our specific focus, our innate beingness radiating its ineffable, yet paradoxically, very tangible essence through our life activity. Our Light is our service, our love, our devotion., our dedication and loyal consistent application of spiritual laws and principles in our thought, words and deeds! Our Light is the demonstration of our gifts, whatever they are or are yet to be. Our Light is our capacity, our talent, our joy and our thankfulness,—"pressed down, shaken together and running over"—as the gates of heaven are opened into and through the doors and windows of our lives!

In honoring our inner radiance, our Sacred Light, the Inner Flame of our God, we have but to choose to look at clarity and not confusion. We have but to focus upon resolution of problems, love of ourselves and others, forgiveness and release instead of fear, woundedness or loss. Our very life then is a daily testimony to the activity of God's Presence! It cannot be lost, buried, destroyed or taken away. No sickness can cover it! No problem can eclipse or hide the true essence of our soul! Death cannot mask it. Pain, hurt or suffering cannot diffuse it. Our Radiance, the Light Within is from everlasting to everlasting!

17

Retreat Into Reality

(Internalizing Spiritual Reality)

"We live, move, and have our being in God....For we are also his offspring." **Acts 17:28**

"This very hour begin to do the work thy spirit glories in. A thousand unseen forces wait to aid. Begin!"
Paul Brunton

∾

In the secular world, some commonly held viewpoints are that life is hard, cruel, unfair. Clichés abound depicting life as a harsh task master, a towering tyrant exacting pain, punishment and ultimately death from every person. We hear statements such as, "No one gets out of life alive!", or "The great equalizer is death."

Is it any wonder, then, that when a truth seeker begins his or her personal journey seeking to discover a new or different reality, or a new and different possibility about the viewpoints about life with which he or she has been "programmed", he or she is in for something of a shocking awakening?

As set forth in the United Nations Charter, we read, "Since wars begin *in the minds of men*, it is *in the minds of men* that the defenses of peace must be constructed." Ernest Holmes, founder of the movement Science of Mind, says it another way, "When we use our creative imagination in strong faith, it will create for us whatever we have formed in thought."

The seeker of truth makes the startling discovery of the possibility that something can be different or better or easier or clearer, that the forces of change begin in his/her mind. That is to say, the process of change begins in the thinking, or in the attitude of the individual about life—*before* a shift or change occurs in the outer world, or as some prefer, the "real world", or the "real life".

Resultingly, this implies personal responsibility for our thoughts, attitudes and beliefs. If change, or at least the possibility for change is in us, then the fault for life's unfairness is mitigated or eased a little. If, indeed, we are the masters of our fate, it is no longer possible to blame an absentee father (or none at all), or an over protective mother, or an alcoholic parent for our inability to cope with life or to make our relationships with spouses, lovers, children or friends work.

Additionally, lack of opportunity is not controlled by outside circumstances as much as by inside feelings or perceptions of ourselves or of others. Rather, it is our fears that restrict us. Franklin Delano Roosevelt, 32nd president of the U.S. (1933-45) said, "The only thing we have to fear is fear itself," thereby stating a great teaching without calling it spiritual or universal as such.

If we live, move and have our being in God as the Bible teaches, this suggests that our real nature is sacred. Our essence is sacred, holy. The life force that flows through us is sacred, full of promise, full of splendor, pregnant with infinite possibility, opportunity and potential. This would seem to imply that *perceptions* about life as being unfair, hurtful or unjust are incomplete perceptions. They are based on faulty observations, or inaccurate assessments of our involvements with life.

When we accept that we can change our lives by changing our self limiting attitudes, by changing our restrictive beliefs about what life is or is not, we take a giant step forward in creating a new reality for ourselves, and for others as well. A subtle change in attitude about a problematic job, or boss or peer can open doors for improved working conditions. A shift in belief from holding a view such as "Life is hard work; blood, sweat and tears", to *"Life is responding to my new perception that all that I do prospers,"* will produce significant change in all aspects of one's life. Certainly, it will produce a change in our attitudinal approach to money and finances and ultimately in our actual experience of more income, improved benefits or a promotion in the marketplace.

Whatever our individual religious affiliation or identification, we must each eventually come to realize that limits in our life's expression are self imposed; restrictions are thoughts or idea barriers awaiting our decision for removal. Our retreat into reality is an accepting of our cocreative work with life. If we are God's offspring (Acts 17:28), we must, somehow, come to accept God is our life. God indwells all life and lives through us. As our life, God is not harsh, or unjust or unfair. God is not cruel, punishing or limiting. It is rather that we are misperceiving God's plan or purpose for us within the context of our life.

Retreating into reality is not about denying our pain or pretending that woundedness or suffering doesn't exist. Rather, it suggests that we move through it, look beyond pain and hurt to the real source of our being. In the vernacular of today, we might say, "If life hands you a lemon, make lemonade!"

Affirming life can be the greatest opportunity and experience we will ever have to discover who we are. This is not a "pie in the sky" attitude, but rather a major shift in thought from perceiving limits as walls to seeing walls as opportunities for making new approaches to life, as opportunities for creative thinking and innovative solutions.

Perhaps the Biblical story of the walls of the city of Jericho in the Old Testament holds a promise for our change in consciousness. The seven priests compassed the city of Jericho seven days (once each day for 6 days and 7 times on the last day). The priests blew on trumpets, the people shouted and the walls fell (Joshua 6:1-27). So we, through diligence, spiritual practices, adhering to disciplines such as prayer, meditation, et cetera, will move beyond the "walls" of doubt, fear, loss, anger, greed, selfishness and pride and become open to, retreat into the reality of God's promise of unlimited good!

18

Camelot - Dreams of Perfection

"The rain may never fall til after sundown. By eight the morning fog must disappear. In short, there's simply not a more congenial spot for happ'ly-ever-aftering than here in Camelot!" **Lerner and Loewe**

"The perfected man does not interfere in the life of beings. He does not impose himself on them, but he 'helps all beings to their freedom.'"
Lao-Tse - Martin Buber

∾

Perhaps one of man's deepest yearnings is to reach an *ultimate* state of knowing and perfection on the spiritual level, and achievement and accomplishment in the physical world. From ancient to present day societies there have been those individuals and groups who have sought to establish communities that would embody an utopian ideal, places where people could live together in shared communal environments. Such communities have been focused toward specific visions of equality of wealth, equally shared responsibilities, equal opportunities for learning, creativity and recreation, as well as for spiritual growth and development.

During the 1960's, for example, we witnessed the resurgent development of communes or communities of composite "families". They purportedly subscribed to ideals which embraced equality of the sexes and shared responsibilities. It was their intent that they might help to create a "Camelot", an example of what an ultimate state of perfection might be like in a "darkened world".

Though the dreams and goals of the communes never quite achieved reality, the desire for a "Camelot", a place where ideals and ideologies, creativity and capabilities, purpose and playfulness could mutually coexist, still continues to surface the world over. What we need to learn, however, is that attempting to create perfection on the outer level is "putting the cart before the horse".

Spiritual teachers the world over have revealed that the kingdom of God is within us. Jesus said, *"The kingdom of God cometh not with observation: Neither shall they say, Lo here! or, lo there! for, behold, the kingdom of God is within you."* (St. Luke 17:20-21) This would suggest, perhaps, that before attempting to create an outer utopia (Camelot) filled with our composite dreams, wishes and desires, it might be wiser to begin to create an inner world that is filled with clarity: a clear sense of purpose, direction, love and beauty. As St. Paul said, *"Whatsoever things are just,...are pure,...are lovely,...are of good report: if there be any virtue,...any praise, think on these things."* (Philippians 4:8)

One of our most difficult lessons, or most difficult tasks is to realize the ancient truth, "As above, so below." Or, we might say, "As it is within us, so it is expressed outside of us." The desire for perfection is, ultimately, the yearning to know, to have a meaningful, direct experience of God, or Source. The striving for perfection in all areas of our lives (our physical, emotional, mental and spiritual arenas) is perhaps our Divine Self urging us to *do* more, *be* more, to keep reaching and allowing ourselves to deepen and expand. First comes the *idea* of growth, movement or possibility. Here we see *First Cause*, to be! To be more!

It is when we begin to respond to that inner urging "to be" that we begin to seek to discover our personal relationship to Source, God, Infinite Being, Life. We begin by beginning. We start with our inner work (prayer, meditation, contemplation, reflection, self-examination) and, as we are consistent, clarity about who we are slowly emerges. As we pray or meditate we discover God's Presence, we feel connected to something larger than ourselves, bigger than our egos or our (petty or insignificant) attitudes, preferences, viewpoints or concerns. Contemplation, reflection, self-examination enables us to move past or through our issues to see the bigger picture, the larger dream, the grander vision, the "Camelot" we seek. In other words, we begin by doing the work on ourselves and our lives from right where we are—*first!* Then, as we honor our inner nature—the virtues, talents, skills and abilities—we can move to actualize them, or demonstrate them in form in the physical world. This process is known as the act of manifestation. "Camelot", then, is not just a dream image nor a fantasy of a fanciful world of make believe. It is a profound possibility. It is our personal image to actualize from the depths of our being.

To create a dream of perfection means, at a deeper level, to be aware that God's Power and Presence are truly *available* to us—from the innermost depths of our being. His Power is ours to use as we are able to do so wisely, with pure intentionality, with love, integrity, clear vision—with an ever deepening sense of purpose and direction.

It will only be after we have some degree of control (mastery) of our physical-mental-emotional nature, tempered and balanced by an awareness of the indwelling Presence, that we can then focus on our outer life to make our contribution, to offer our gifts, to sing our song, to help create our world. We can then help to make our planet safer, our environment healthier, our cities, towns and villages places of sanctity, special beauty, harmony and healing.

"Camelot" is in truth peopled with real princes and princesses, kings and queens—*now! Everyone* is a royal person. You are. I am. We all are. That realization comes to each of us when we discover our relationship to the Source. Utopia is here, now, if we can but accept it. It is not delayed to some special event such as the mystical Brigadoon, the magical village that appears only for a day once every hundred years, where life is harmonious and happy, where war is unknown, no one ages and death never occurs.

Our "Camelot" is filled with opportunities to *live*—in the real world—daily, weekly, yearly, out of a place within our being that awaits to support and celebrate that process. Life awaits! We can live it from a place of fullness, courage, trust and a willingness to risk the effort to bring our dreams into reality.

This special place is not fairyland, or Disney World, Shangri-La or a return to the primal Garden of Eden. It is structured upon the foundation of our learning to take responsibility for who *we*, individually, experience ourselves to be. Today is the day to begin. To do so brings joy, aliveness and freedom. Those who have gone before us and continue to celebrate life offer us support and encouragement as we unfold our own processes—our own efforts to find perfection —"Camelot!"

"Camelot" is here, right where you are, right now. Can't you hear the trumpets sounding announcing the banquet that has been prepared for you, in your honor! Listen ...

19

Abundance Everywhere

"The whole of creation exists in you and it is your destiny to become increasingly aware of its infinite wonders and to experience ever greater portions of it." **Neville**

∾

In a world of much mass confusion, contradictions and endless conflicts, the belief—no, perhaps even the very concept—that abundance is an actuality everywhere present can give the impression of being astounding and profound on one hand, and ridiculous and foolish on the other. Comparing third world countries, whose peoples live in abject poverty, to America where wealth appears to flow freely (alongside serious poverty also), promises of abundance or prosperity would seem to be outrageous.

Apparent contradictions notwithstanding, ancient and modern teachers alike suggest that there are principles and universal laws that govern abundance (prosperity), or its lack. It behooves the serious student of metaphysics to explore these principles and gain some measure of insight and understanding for their fuller life's expression.

Jesus, the Christ said, *"I am come that they might have life and that they might have it more abundantly."* (John 10:10) What a magnificent promise! For many religious minded people, however, this promise is inconsistent with the (conflicting) teachings about (the vow of) poverty, denial and suffering. How can we approach it then?

Abundance is defined as, "an overflowing supply or quantity—fullness, affluence, wealth." From a Truth perspective, or a larger, broader viewpoint (including metaphysical), abundance is *already* ours. It is a matter of first "knowing" it, then "claiming" it and, finally, "demonstrating" it.

1. Knowing abundance suggests that Universal Intelligence gives us wealth in terms of *ideas*. Here we discover the concept that we are worthy, valuable and important in the universal scheme of things. Remember this affirmation: "God loves me and approves of me."

Slowly, perhaps, we will begin to recognize that we have good, useful and creative ideas that can be implemented and put to work. Knowing implies discerning and studying truth teachings. Knowing imparts the law or teaching that what we are within, we are without. What we hold (know) in consciousness, we show forth (exemplify) in our affairs.

2. Claiming our abundance suggests the process or activity necessary to move us toward step #3, "demonstrating". In truth teachings, claiming our good is actually the process of affirmation and visualization. Additionally, it is verbalizing as a statement of truth that that which we desire is possible of realization. First, it is the consistent practice of all of step #1 above and then visualizing abundance, success and our good flowing into our lives from all sources and all directions. It is the blended activity of our feeling and mental nature united into a composite. As we claim prosperity "inside" our beingness, *and,* actually accept God's promise that we are deserving and worthy, we are then ready to demonstrate our abundance!

3. Demonstrating suggests bringing into a form (manifesting) that which we are seeking. We move, a step at a time, in the direction of our goals. We remain open to life, to opportunity. A new career. A better job. Improved health. Healing in our body or in our lives. A better or perhaps a new relationship. Peace of mind. Freedom from pain, stress, hurt or abuse. As we manifest or make real (tangible, touchable, solid) our good, we will next discover that the mental equivalent of plenty that we hold inwardly, unfolds outwardly in our affairs and the events that compose our lives. To the degree that we are able to decisively follow through with steps #1 through #3, we will see results!

Abundance everywhere exists then in *our* consciousness, as well as in the consciousness of *others*. We must never allow ourselves to say, "he/she has more opportunities than I, better circumstances, more privileges, richer parents, etc., etc." It may be externally true that others have more accumulated wealth or good in their lives at the moment. Yet, our abundance cannot come forward, unfold and manifest *in us* if we focus upon what others have, have done or are doing, and not upon what we also have but have not yet claimed or learned how to demonstrate!

We are each a child of God. Everyone we meet, from pauper to prince, from the super brilliant to the most humble, illiterate fellow sojourner, all share in the same ocean of consciousness. Everyone gifts us with hope, inspiration and opportunities to learn, grow, deepen, awaken and unfold. Creative ideas are ours at every turn. Choices await *our* decision.

Let us never underestimate ourselves! Loss or failure is never final. It means that we have tried and must try again and do things differently the next time! Choose to ask for clearer vision, a brighter picture, a better idea, a stronger relationship.

Abundance is not just about wealth or the accumulation of things, or "toys" or fancy baubles. It is about the owning (knowing, claiming and demonstrating) of our celestial birthright. An abundance attitude is seeing opportunity arise out of failure or loss. An abundance consciousness unfolds when we can go past our limits and see the starlight, the sunlight and the light of heaven beyond the rubble at our feet.

In closing, I would like to share a story told by Norman Vincent Peale, printed in *Plus, The Magazine of Positive Thinking*.

"We will know our attitude is on the right tract when we are like the small businessman whose clothing store was threatened with extinction. A national chain store had moved in and acquired all the properties on his block. This one particular businessman refused to sell. 'All right then, we'll build all around you and put you out of business', the new competitors said. The day came when the small merchant found himself hemmed in with a new department store stretching out on both sides of his little retail shop. The competitors' banner announced, 'Grand Opening!' The merchant countered with a banner stretching across the entire width of his store. It read, 'Main Entrance'."

20

The Wonderful World Within

"Know ye not that ye are the Temple of God, and that the Spirit of God dwelleth in you?" **1 Corinthians 3:16**

∾

Over 4,000 years ago, in one of the oldest civilizations known to mankind, there lived a sage by the name of Yu. Yu was a learned man and the founder of the first dynasty of Chinese emperors. Of an evening, Yu would gather his students together in the courtyard of his palace and teach them how to live effectively. "Follow what is right," he said, "and you will be fortunate; do not follow it, and you will be unfortunate ... the results of life are but the shadows and echoes of your thoughts and acts."

Perhaps the greatest mystery in life is that all that we know, learn and amass in our churches, institutes and great halls of higher learning, or from teachers, friends, scientists and parents is not true knowing after all. The great intellectual assessments about life are based on observation, study, analysis and then, finally, synthesis. We carefully examine the world of nature, the habits of animals, birds, or even human kind. We scrutinize the pieces of information thus gleaned and then make careful, considered evaluations and calculations based upon such data. Interesting, intriguing and informative though this may be, it is highly interpretive and not useful in discerning the inner truth of who we are.

Learning about our real selves is exciting; it may even be thrilling and at times enthralling. It involves, as Tara Singh has succinctly stated, "There is nothing to seek, only to undo." Discovery about the inner world emerges in many ways. Let us examine here briefly some of the approaches useful in enabling us to explore the inward way of knowing who we are.

1. **Prayer**—to enter into spiritual communion with God or an object of worship. Prayer leads us into the Unknown, the Inner Sanctuary. It has many forms, but essentially prayer enables the supplicant to discover the active power of God's Presence, which is available at the very moment of prayer.

2. **Meditation**—to be open to, receptive to, attuned to the transcendent dimensions; to ponder, to be able to reflect on the pure nature of being. Here, when properly attuned, we can "hear" the still, small voice of God. It is here that we become aware, consciously, of transformation and healing. It is here that the "light of a thousand suns" illumines the spark of Divine Light within our own being.

3. **Study** of Sacred Writings - Ancient teachers as well as "modern" mystics of the Inner Way advise us to study the written, classical spiritual teachings. Some of these include the Bible, the Torah, the Koran, the Bhagavad Gita, the Vedas, the writings of Lao-tze, Buddha and Confucius. There are many other sacred writings and highly respected ancient and modern texts that can be useful for reflection, contemplation and the deepening of insight into our real nature. Study aligns us to our Larger Self, the Transcendent Reality. Study enables us to examine what the inspired revelators have given us and thus, ultimately, to come to know something of the spiritual truth about who we are.

4. **Practice** of disciplines such as yoga, fasting and other physical/emotional/mental processes helps the individual to purify the body, purge the ego nature, cleanse the desire makeup that cloud or interfere with the soul's larger purpose. Discipline clarifies, focuses energy, eliminates fragmentation in one's life and aids the aspirant to become truly receptive to his or her Soul Nature.

The wonderful world within becomes more accessible to us the more we accept the promise of our personal potential. For example, if we accept that we have an ability to write, or act, or paint, or design things, we automatically give ourselves permission to utilize our creative talents. The more we act upon our creative impulses, the more we fulfill our potential. The deeper we tap into our creative reservoir, the more we discover the limitless dimensions of the world within. Our creativity will literally keep opening up, expanding and unfolding. It emerges from within in a flow of living waters of Life—the Source.

The Bible says that we are made in the image and likeness of God. If this is true, we coexist with a Power higher and greater than we usually feel in ourselves. When we experience difficulty, the little self of us forever seeks to solve things on the outside—by manipulating people and pushing around the world of effects. Unfortunately, this often creates frustration, unhappiness and grief for everyone concerned. However, the answer to every problem already lies within us. Why is this? Because God as Love, Light, Life, Energy and Intelligence is the very basis of our being, and God is with us at every moment. Thus, we can consciously open ourselves to the voice of Intuition, which will guide us unerringly into a healing Oneness of perfect right action, right where we are.

As we learn to surrender, to let go and let the Wisdom and Power that is God within us, guide us and sustain us, we realize our Oneness with God. We become conscious cocreators with Life Itself, wherein all things are possible. We are filled to overflowing in the eternal here and now.

21

Positive Thinking - Expanding Into the Big Picture

"Be not conformed to this world: But be ye transformed by the renewing of your mind, that ye may prove what is that good and acceptable, and perfect will of God."
Romans 12:2

∾

Allowing for the diversity of possible circumstances and conditions in our individual lives, in our interests and pursuits, we are, nevertheless, "bombarded" with specifically targeted images in the media (newspapers, magazines, television, etc.) which seek to evoke a favorable (positive) response from us. Advertisers, for example, seek to influence us to purchase their product by oftentimes promising "new dimensions" for our lives if we will but use their mouthwash, or deodorant, detergent, gasoline, motor oil, or whatever. I'm sure you can add hundreds of examples of your own. The point being, in the multidimensional marketplace of the world, whether it's a product to market, an idea to communicate, a concept or a cause to ignite, a movement to push, etc., etc., the advertisers and promoters are, for all intents and purposes, coming from a place of confidence or positivity.

We must individually decide (wisely, hopefully) whether or not the products, concepts, ideas, "opportunities", promises, etc., are appropriate for us and therefore useful or meaningful.

Positive thinking is the *process* of creating a viewpoint that is confident, constructive and sure. Positive thinking may therefore require of us a different perception or viewpoint than we now have, or previously held, that is free of limitations or barriers.

In the area of healing, for example, suppose we somehow injure an arm. We might react by both mentally taking a picture of the injury and physically and emotionally feeling the pain. Positive thinking suggests that we allow ourselves to mentally take a new picture of the injury. One suggestion is to see it (image it) as healing. We picture the bruise disappearing, the cut closing, the injury healing to a state of wholeness, the arm well and strong. Positive thinking also suggests (by implication and understanding) that we also feel the pain lessen and release. In other words, through the process of visualization, we learn how to change our perception from hurt and pain to a sense of wholeness and freedom from restrictions.

Louise Hay suggests in her highly regarded book *You Can Heal Your Life* that positive, loving, nurturing feelings and images are the basic building blocks of effective changes in the chemistry of the body to heal itself! She goes on to suggest the daily use of affirmations to help bring change.

Affirmations are usually short, very upbeat statements that we repeat aloud or silently over and over to ourselves. Some examples: "*I Trust the process of life. All I need is always taken care of. I am safe.*" ... "*I am well, whole and strong. The Life of God flows through me wherever I am. All is complete and divine order is in my life* ***now****!*"

Norman Vincent Peale, author of the famous book *The Power of Positive Thinking*, introduced a concept that shocked the fundamental Christian viewpoint. He suggested that although God is the healer, the Source of all life, we *individually* can and must take responsibility for our lives by the *way, manner* and *attitude* of our thinking! Metaphysicians have long known the truth of this teaching and many have successfully applied it to their individual life situations.

What, then, does this imply for us? It suggests that even as all kinds of businesses, large and small institutions, and hosts of individual societies and organizations are applying the principle of positive thinking in their structuring and functioning, so we, too, as awakening spiritual beings can incorporate these ideas into our expanding personal lives, into the big picture of who and what we truly are.

1. **Be an example of positive thinking.** When you are faced with a challenge, a conflict, or a difficulty, choose to see (image) the challenge met, the conflict resolved, or the difficulty surmounted. First visualize the positive possibilities —then feel them being accomplished—and finally, *act* in a way that moves in the direction of the positive, desired resolution.

2. **Realize life is an ongoing process.** The inner work of changing habits of thinking, of being open to a new or different viewpoint may take time. Begin today where you are. Observe your reactions, your impulses, and if you are not coming from a place of affirmation for yourself or another, try immediately to reverse your reactions or impulses to fit into the big picture. Haphazard or halfhearted efforts won't produce significant results. Be willing to be consistent and disciplined.

3. **Support your life with positive interests, activities and people.** Choose positive books, movies, places to visit. Become active in an inspiring church. Commit yourself to others from a place of love, but not duty ... from a place of giving, but not obligation. Allow yourself to have fun, relax and enjoy your experience of life as it unfolds for you.

Give your best, to yourself, to others, to life. No lukewarm, indifferent efforts. No quasi-excited involvements. Give quality time, effort and service. Whatever you do, do well and unstintingly. The more you give of your best, the more powerful, positive and rewarding your experience of life will be.

Thus, positive thinking leads one away from doubt, fear and loss, from a sense of separation and hurt into the deepening awareness that our life is always an opportunity to grow and deepen, to expand and unfold, to awaken to ever greater heights/depths of our being into the big picture. We thus claim ever more fully the heritage and destiny of all our soul's yearnings!

22

The Miracle of God's Love

"Beloved, if God so loved us, we ought also to love one another." **1 John 4:11**

∾

From the tiniest blade of grass to the most distant star within the cosmos, all of the universe teems with radiant life. This life pulse energizes, supports, strengthens and coexists within all life forms. Man shares this connection and is himself able to give expression to this pulse in a variety of ways, both subtly and overtly, as he awakens to the realization of his own inner nature.

Awakening is the real inner purpose of our life. To awaken signifies the process we individually grow through in discovering the internal as well as external perimeters or boundaries of our nature. It is the experiencing of our real selves as opposed to our illusory, or ego superficial selves which normally rules our daily or our outer life.

How is this awakening accomplished? A perimeter is discovered usually when we meet resistance to some proposed direction we seek to explore or learn about. We also discover a perimeter when we "try our wings" on a project or attempt to accomplish something new we have never tried before and meet with unexpected success or expansion. The nature of the discovery of perimeters allows us to learn about those areas of ourselves that teach us how we can honor, incorporate, integrate and thus own our very deepest qualities, talents, skills or abilities.

Another kind of perimeter is the kind of experience we have with another human being in relationships. Any kind of relationship teaches us as much about our own person as it reveals about that other being. The stresses and strains, the tugs, pulls and stretchings that allow both intimate and friendship relationships to work create yet another framework or dimension for our growth. This occurs when we find ourselves either attracted to or repulsed by specific people, be they family members, loved ones, friends, acquaintances, or people we have just met. The attraction-repulsion process is part of the discovery we make about ourselves which helps us to learn about the real nature of our being. In essence, that real nature is more than, or is greater than, the discovery of the tugs and pulls of the emotional fabric of the personality self, the ego self, that part of our self that "likes" or "dislikes" anything or anyone.

Perhaps the greatest challenge is to accept that our inner nature, or our sacred, holy essence is already perfect, whole and complete. The meaning of love, metaphysically speaking, is to be open, receptive, and attuned to the flow and rhythm of our individual life process. Openness is synonymous with acceptance or receptivity. It is the permission we give to ourselves and our experience. It is the discoveries we make from our experiences that enable us to know the dimensions and regions of love that exist and are ever available to us.

God's love is not some vague hoped-for state of being available only to a select, favored few. It is already ours just for the claiming of it, and the accepting, honoring, and owning of our real being. Awakening, then, is in part a discovery of the Miracle of God's Love as being ever accessible to us wherever we are and whatever may be happening in our lives.

It is not enough to merely know that God's love exists or is possible. It must become our personal experience within our lives. We must fill our heart, soul and body with Divine Love by claiming it and accepting it. Then we must think about it, feel it, show it, radiate it, give it and accept it, demonstrate it everywhere we go, in all that we do, say think and feel.

Truly, life cannot have meaning, purpose or value unless we are willing to give Life the joyous gift of our beingness, our true self. We make such a gift when we cease to criticize, when we cease our grumbling, faultfinding, nursing of grievances, thinking and emotional projections of negative energies. These are fatal to the demonstration of Divine Love which would heal us and allow us to integrate our lives and become whole.

Awakening is a rich, vibrant, loving demonstration of the soul's journey to the stars. It is the heartfelt embrace of the Spirit singing as we seek for fuller and fuller expression of all that we are. It is the call of our deepest urges, our most powerful yearnings to reach out and touch that which is the highest and best within us and within life. It is our thrust toward God that allows us to become who we are. And in that becoming, we own, honor, accept and demonstrate the holy and healing Presence called Love.

The following is quoted from *Emmet Fox's Golden Keys to Successful Living* by Herman Wolhorn:

"My soul is filled with Divine Love. I am surrounded by Divine Love. I radiate Love and Peace to the whole world. I have conscious Divine Love. God is Love, and there is nothing in existence but God and His Self-expression. All men are expressions of Divine Love; therefore, I can meet with nothing but the expressions of Divine Love. Nothing ever takes place but the Self-expressing of Divine Love.

"All this is true now.... I do not have to try to bring this about, but I observe it already in being now. Divine Love is the actual nature of Being. There is only Divine Love, and I know this.

"I perfectly understand what Divine Love is. I have conscious realization of Divine Love. The Love of God burns in me for all humanity. I am a lamp of God, radiating Divine Love to all whom I meet, to all whom I think of.

"I forgive everything that can possibly need forgiveness—positively everything. Divine Love fills my heart, and all is well. I now radiate Love to the whole universe, excluding no one. I experience Divine Love. I demonstrate Divine Love.

"I thank God for this."

23

A Rainbow of Thankfulness

"He which soweth sparingly shall reap sparingly; and he which soweth bountifully shall reap bountifully."

2 Corinthians 9:6

∾

Every life contains within it a mixture of experiences which can be weighed favorably or unfavorably. The tendency is for the average person to focus upon his experiences from a restricted viewpoint. The result is that the greater picture of life escapes him. His restricted viewpoint is like wearing blinders and such a person is "locked in" to a life of mediocrity, hurt and frustration. However, when we shift our focus from fear, limitation and loss and view life in a more positive, powerful light, we can realize tremendous accomplishments, healing and renewal.

Six years ago a dear friend suffered a major heart attack which resulted in an extended hospitalization and a long recuperation period. The business he ran, a small family operated store, failed. Debts climbed and though his wife and family were very supportive, he sank into a severe decline, a deep depression. Ultimately he lost everything he and his family had acquired.

During his darkest moments, in the midst of great pain and hurt, he had a dream in which he was "told" that God had a great work ahead for him. The dream suggested the he move his family to California and to begin to study for the ministry. He had many choices to make. Six months after his heart attack, he borrowed money from his brother and moved himself and his family to Los Angeles. In time he found work in the aerospace industry. He enrolled in school at the headquarters of the United Church of Religious Science in Los Angeles.

Today he is an ordained minister, a healing practitioner and has a new life. He is whole, well and vital. His ministry is flourishing. He is growing and successful. What began as tragedy, loss and severe restriction has been converted into positive redirection and triumph! The actuality of his heart attack did not change, but what did was that he chose to view those circumstances and to redirect his energies in a useful and positive manner.

Our lives are constantly demonstrating how we use or direct our personal energies. Remarkable, life changing events can happen when we *make up our mind* to achieve a certain purpose or proceed in a certain direction. Deep forces from within impel us to produce, to achieve or to create the thing we have decided upon. The choice, however, is always ours to make. We decide the direction of our lives...constantly!

Thanksgiving, or the act of being thankful, is an inner state which acknowledges the Source of all good as our constant supply. This internal thankful state of our being actually enables and empowers us. As we express our gratitude to the Source in prayer or in the quietude of meditation, we open to the deepest parts of our own nature and begin to connect with or link with, those areas in ourselves *and in the universe* that are unlimited and unrestricted! That connection frees us from the dependency upon outer circumstances, appearances or conditions. Genuine thanksgiving (at-one-ment) then flows from our deepest inner dimensions into all aspects of our life and allows us to demonstrate the spiritual principle "Whatsoever a man soweth, that shall he also reap".

Living in the world, the outer physical dimensionality, is an opportunity to grow more conscious of who and what we are, to awaken to our true spiritual nature. If we attempt to work, live, move, think and act in a positive and supportive manner regarding our life experiences, we ultimately discover that the connectedness we seek is available and that God's unlimited good is unfolding and emerging in our life in Divine order.

Certainly physical existence offers plenty of hurt, frustration and challenge. Certainly there is much evidence of lack, poverty and all manner of disease, pain and suffering.

Our challenge is, not to add to what exists (not to give strength to "appearances"), but to shift our focus from feelings of loss and woundedness to feelings of acceptance of the Presence of God's Healing Love. With acceptance comes confidence. As confidence builds, strength and conviction arise and grow. We reap bountifully from the actual step by step changes we make in our own lives.

The attitude and state of being of thankfulness become a vital and magnificent expression of our life that opens the door of greater good. As others have an experience of us as being more open and receptive, they in turn become open, allowing, giving and yielding. Opportunities, gifts, benefits of many kinds flow into our lives. A rainbow of thankfulness emerges in our lives out of the deepening contact and the profound sense of God's Presence that guides and directs, nurtures and sustains us wherever we are and what ever we may be doing.

24

On the Threshold of Light

"Always remember one thing: God is not far from you and you are not far from God." **Swami Muktananda**

∾

In all ancient traditions, secular and non-secular alike, references to the existence or emanation of light consistently reappear. Light is, at once, both an inner quality ascribed to regions of the soul or the Divine Spirit within man, or it is perceived to source from some distant star or central sun at the center of the universe.

Mysterious, transparent, ever-changing, light is ever the subject of both the scientist and the mystic. From the hidden domain of the center of the most minute particles of the atom to the philosophic, symbolic, metaphysical utterances of poets, the substance or essence of light remains just that. It is always an essence, always present, always somehow beckoning to us like the welcome flashes of flame dancing to greet the weary traveler at a hearthside, or a single burning candle shedding its radiance to all who behold it.

Dr. Elizabeth Kubler Ross, Ph.D., writes in her book *Death, the Final Stage of Growth*, and Raymond Moody, M.D., concurs in his book *Life After Life*, that "light appears beyond or through a tunnel", describing what people have reported who have survived near-death experiences as they individually passed through the door that separates the physical world from the spiritual dimensions—and returned.

What is this light that emerges through us? What is the significance of this energy that defies description except in scientific language? (The dictionary defines light as "an electromagnetic radiation that has a wave length in the range from about 3900 to about 7700 angstrom that may be perceived by the unaided, normal human eye".)

In the Quaker tradition, the Light is the guiding spirit or divine Presence in every being. The Hindu scriptures speak of the Inner Light, the sacred essence of God present in all mankind and coexisting in all form. The Bible tells us *"Ye are children of the light, and children of the day..."* (1 Thessalonians 5:5), suggesting that the inner qualities of the spirit (light) are available and accessible to *all* people.

Indeed, it appears that everywhere we are, the Source of Life is ever available, ever present, ever near. In a very real, personal and practical sense, it suggests that God's Presence is not something we must hope for, beg for or plead for. It is already ours. We must allow ourselves to become open and receptive to It in every area of our life. The light, or inner essence of God is readily available to us! Again, all we must do is ask! "Behold, I stand at the door and knock; and, if any man open I will come in and sup with him." (Revelation 3:20) And again, Jesus himself stated (in John 8:12), "I am the light of the world; he who follows me will not walk in darkness, but will have the light of life."

Our task is to walk on the threshold of light. We accomplish this in several principal ways:

First, accepting the truth about our life, that God is emerging in us and as our experience of life. In acceptance of life's experience, we move into the deep, quiet, inner knowledge of our real nature and past the appearances of lack or limitation.

Second, we leave the past in the past! To know the real truth of ourselves we must gently lay aside the hurts, woundedness and broken bits and pieces of all our yesterdays. To keep thinking about past experiences energizes them. Do we really want the old patterns, the fears, the failures and disappointments back? This step is also called forgiveness or release!

Third, move in the direction of the desired good! So many cannot enter the threshold of light because they constantly question themselves, each other, other people and, ultimately, God whether or not their good is coming. Is it really going to work? Will their needs be met? Will they really get the job? Will their health really improve? The wisdom teachings all agree on this point: We must accept our good as manifesting now and keep moving in the direction of the desired result!

The Light is not something we reach for in mystical states of awareness, or seek for in answer to prayer. It is not a sudden vision filled with pulsating emanations of light energy or a prophetic revelation. The inner light is more the sense we have of the Holy, Divine, Sacred Presence that undergirds all form, all things, all people, all life experience.

To see the light either visually through normal physical vision or internally might be interpreted to signify that there is a connecting Presence that is Sourcing all life forms. And, that our duty is to become conscious of our personal relationship to that light, that power, that deep area of our being and recognize that indeed, we are children of the light!

As you stand on the threshold of light—wherever you are in your own consciousness—may the Source of that Light ennoble your life and fill it with the Peace that passes understanding.

25

Explorations in Inner Space

"Jesus answered him, 'Truly, truly I say unto you, unless one is born anew, he cannot see the kingdom of God'." **John 3:3**

∾

In our search for the gaining of spiritual wisdom, we are lead into many pathways and perhaps into sometimes strange, curious, and/or appealing philosophies or approaches to Inner Truth or inner space. There are those who promote themselves as teachers (legitimately or not) who promise everything from instantaneous enlightenment, life changing transformations, and lasting inner peace, to special spiritual powers or gifts, psychic revelations, regenerations from disease, and healing or recovery from all manner of physical, emotional, mental and psychological imbalances. The list could go on. The genuine exists side-by-side with the fraudulent and sensational. Adherents are drawn to both the real and the unreal and confusion abounds.

Perhaps the most difficult to understand aspect of any approach to the Inner Path is to recognize that each major philosophy is based upon the teaching or knowledge of some ancient spiritual tradition. While this in itself is not difficult to accept, a problem is presented when a self-styled teacher suggests or proclaims that his "inner guidance:" has revealed a "new" system or philosophy, a totally "new teaching" never before given on earth!

This "new" teaching may promise a panacea for total living: victory over illness, mastery over business and personal relationships, along with many "new techniques" to acquire *all* you desire—power, wealth, fame, special gifts of spiritual value. The truth seeker is confronted with a dilemma.

Does one accept the *new* philosophy and discard the old tradition, or does one try to combine some watered-down ingredients of both?

In reply, let me make my position quite clear. Spiritual wisdom is acquired by the acknowledgment of the inherent power of God, the inner spark of Divinity dwelling within each of us. This acknowledgment, recognition and understanding is gained through the classical approaches to inner wisdom: study of sacred writings, prayer and meditation, and the *application* of the teachings in our daily life.

A new process or system can offer significant insights. A fresh approach to what traditional spiritual teachings offer is healthy and may be stimulating to soul awareness and, therefore, useful to the gaining of spiritual wisdom. The Source is ever revealing Itself anew.

However, so-called techniques that promise transformation in a weekend, enlightenment at the end of a special retreat or training session or as the result of the "anointing" of the seeker by a teacher, guru or visiting "illuminatus" are not to be construed as the gaining of spiritual wisdom.

Some spiritual techniques, if properly practiced, can help to refine the subtle levels of being, such as the thought patterns, the emotional upheavals, and help the physical body to experience a greater state of wellness. The tried and true spiritual techniques, trainings and special energy connections can indeed be useful and helpful to motivate us, inspire us and elevate our consciousness beyond its normal range.

Spiritual gifts are the fruits of spiritual awakening. These gifts emerge in our life as we become more conscious of our soul's potential. An example of this kind of awakening occurs when we tap our inner power through prayer or meditation, or through any appropriate spiritual discipline. It emerges in our life as clearer vision, a deepening sense of purposefulness about our life, more powerful intuition and stronger energies in our talents. An ability to sing is more effective, a skill in writing deepens, a capacity to create as an artist (painter) emerges with more intensity. Soul powers, or *siddhis* (as they are called in the East), also may emerge as psychic revelation, the ability to heal, or the capacity to travel to distant places at the soul level and consciously remember this knowledge upon return to the physical body.

If techniques are offered without appropriate knowledge (grounding) of the teachings from which they are taken, one has no undergirding to support oneself if complications or problems occur. It is absolutely necessary to have the teaching or philosophy that provides the framework, the support and the essence or core of the process, training or experiential approach!

Spiritual wisdom is achieved by learning to integrate all that we have encountered and learned in our life. To be "born anew" suggests a freshness or renewal, perhaps to be transformed completely. Such transformation does not come from a desire to escape life's problems or hurts, its woundedness or despair, but by learning from such experiences all that there is to discover. At the core of all experiences is the "tool" of love—the indwelling God-Consciousness—giving us strength and endurance to surmount and overcome, to balance and transmute the negative into positive. That discovery brings integration or, ultimately, wholeness and a profound deepening of all that we are as human and, in a larger sense, as spiritual beings.

To enter or to "see the kingdom of God" offers us the individual promise to capture the ultimate experience of God's Presence in every area and arena in our life. We do not cling to special techniques or to the glamour of popular teachings which promise a permanent panacea for our life's problems. It is in doing our homework, studying and applying ourselves usefully in life that enables us to be "born anew". Thus it is that we build a more firm foundation and gain a truer perspective in the process of exploring our inner spaces from which we achieve spiritual wisdom.

26

Bridges to Inner Consciousness

"There is ....one God and Father of all, who is above all, and through all and in you all." **Ephesians 4:46**

∾

In our many modes of human expression, a bridge often makes it possible for us to make a connection between one point of land and another, or one point of mind/spirit and another. Such bridges and connections can serve to aid us or empower us to make it possible to accomplish something, or access something which had hitherto been deemed "impossible" or unattainable.

In crossing a large river, a bridge makes the effort of crossing simpler, easier and often much more direct. In our interpersonal relationships, a bridge is often created when we make the initial effort to render service, help or assistance. This may be by trying to help a person overcome a problem or difficulty. Or, we may attempt to help them to broaden their perspective relative to conflicts, issues, or unresolved personal or spiritual matters in their lives.

A bridge suggests a physical or mental structure which crosses a gap. We are lead from one place to another; from one viewpoint to a greater or certainly a different one; from one part of ourselves to a newer or clearer dimension of our being.

How do we create or build a bridge to our Inner Consciousness, our Inner World? Is there any one special way to connect to our Higher Self, to our Divine Nature? Immediate reflection suggests that there must be. Paul says in First Corinthians 12:6, *"And there are diversities of operations, but it is the same God which worketh all in all."* What powerful acknowledgment of God's Indwelling Presence! Indeed, this bridging is demonstrated in a variety of ways some of which are as follows:

Prayer. The opening of our personal life or channel to experience our Larger Selves. This connects with the Christ within us or what is known as the Inner Fire, referred to by the mystics, saints and sages of past and present time.

Meditation. The conscious yielding to the active power of God's Presence within us. Through the various disciplines which quiet the outer mind, we allow ourselves to be open and receptive to our Inner Consciousness. All processes of meditation lead one to make conscious contact with the Inner Consciousness.

Through Study of sacred writings such as the Holy Bible, the Bhagavad Gita, the Koran, the Talmud, the teachings of Lao-Tse, Confucius and other enlightenment teachers and traditions. This leads to both a clarity of spiritual principles and a deepening of those concepts as the framework for our personal awakening to the Inner Christ.

Body-Mind-Spirit. Being consciously and consistently aware of this triune relationship suggests a very practical approach to living: doing our jobs, raising our families, tending to our personal responsibilities and caring for our physical bodies. This means proper foods and nutrition, proper exercise and relaxation. On the mental-emotional level it involves working with and trying to resolve any hurts, guilts, fears, losses, angers and resentments; i.e., utilizing our emotions in healthy and constructive ways. It involves positive and creative uses of our minds and intellects that we may accept, apply and practice what we learn from our experiences to our triune lives.

World service. By finding useful ways to give service to humanity, we become conscious of our at-one-ment with all life. We then stop seeing others as separate from God, from our selves, and we begin to honor them as intricate members of the family of man. As we expand our capacity to give service, we become open to greater connections with life, Inner Consciousness and the lives of others. Thus, as we discover our own wholeness, we also discover that all members of the human race are worthy of our love, our service and our gifts of the Inner Spirit.

Honoring our Inner Process. This means to honor our Inner Connection, our Inner Revelation! Each of us is led into an awareness of the stages we must pass through in order to grow more conscious of who and what we are and what life is all about. For example: one person must heal a wounded, painful relationship with a spouse; another must mend a conflict with a parent, or a child. To effect healing, there are stages (or steps) of work that follow sequentially. As this work is accomplished, revelation comes forth from our Highest Self, our God-Nature, our connection to The Source called the active power of the Holy Spirit! Revelation can come through a dream, through a psychic experience, a vision or a mystical encounter with life which touches the fabric of a miracle either within our own life or that of another. It is here that we experience the Bridges to Inner Consciousness when we come to know human love, or discover the exquisite joy of a newborn child—a glorious sunrise—the gentle face of a dew-kissed rose. It is here in the powerful embrace of life that we discover, that we reach the Christ within!

Although each of the above-outlined Bridges of Inner Consciousness can be discovered or practiced separately, the more one seeks wholeness with the entire being, the more complete and thus more profound will the experience become. Since we do not exist in a vacuum, but rather are inseparably connected at the very deepest level of our beings, we finally come to terms with our own life. We see that everyone on earth can really be helpful to everyone else. Helpful here does not mean doing the inner or outer work for others, nor does it imply control of or over them. Being helpful affords us the opportunity to *consciously give* from the place of love, acceptance and fullness rather than from lack, limitation or restriction.

Creating the bridge to our Inner Consciousness is a process which cannot be pushed by prayer alone, or muscled by meditation, stimulated by drugs, or stormed by arming oneself with book knowledge. It is structured by our willingness to seek that connection openly and unfailingly, to heed the yearnings that arise from the deepest parts of ourselves, and to learn from all that our life affords us. Our Inner Being is always revealing more of itself to us. Our Inner Consciousness is not withheld from us nor is it unfolding conditionally in our life. Often we become frightened or restricted by the ego demands we place upon life. Or, we become distracted by the myriad wants, wishes, needs and compulsions that sidetrack us from our real purpose.

Each soul upon the planet can make his/her connection to the Bridges of Inner Consciousness more possible by utilizing the tools of their triune body-mind-spiritual nature. A bridge does not really serve anyone unless we cross over it or use it. The many ways of accessing our Inner Consciousness that are available to us cannot really be significantly useful unless we choose to act. We must pursue those avenues that teach, inspire and motivate us to try to reach for more. It is that effort to know more, to feel more, to seek for more that enables us to grasp the very Hand of God leading us forward in the steps of our journey to find and own our true self. With Paul, again, we can say with awareness, clarity and profound insight, *"Know ye not that ye are the Temple of God, and that the spirit of God dwelleth in you?"* (1 Corinthians 3:16)

27

Opening Our Hearts and Our Lives to the Christ

"Behold, I stand at the door and knock; and, if any man open, I will come in and sup with him."
Revelation 3:20

"I and the Father are one; I am in him and he is in me...I dwell in you, and you in me...I am the vine and you are the branches." **John 10:30,38; 15:5**

∾

To live with conscious awareness that there is a Divine Presence within our deepest, innermost nature is enormously empowering, comforting and revealing. However, accessing this dimension of our Inner Self is the greatest challenge and the most significant opportunity of our individual life expression.

The Spirit, the "Atman", the "Image of God" in each of us is really the essential core of our own authentic being. Yet, it is rarely experienced by the majority of people who, for the most part, suspend their consciousness in ordinary or earthly states of mundane, day to day awareness and involvement.

Enlightened beings, great saints and mystics, however, have written about their experiences after they have learned to dwell in, function and operate out of "superconscious" levels of mind in which they have contacted the Spirit.

In ancient Sanskrit texts, the superconscious level of mind was called the "buddhi" and anyone who lived in it or was able to maintain a conscious connection to it was called a "buddha". Similarly, in the Judeo-Christian tradition, one who was "anointed" by the Spirit of God was called "an anointed one". In Hebrew "an anointed one" is "a messiah"; and, in Greek this is translated as "a Christ".

Opening our hearts and our lives to Christ is a matter of first becoming aware that we are indeed connected to the Eternal Christ. One way to think about this relationship is to reflect on the words of Jesus; *"I and my Father are one; I am in him and he is in me..."* The Father is the Divine Spirit, God Essence, Innermost Self, Holy Spark! That knowledge is *essential* to our acceptance of it. All wisdom teachings and spiritual traditions speak of this acceptance as being the very basis or core of Self discovery.

Once we come to see that we are part of the greater body of God (the Father), we can begin to acknowledge the connection Jesus (The Christ) had. Jesus not only understood his Divine Connection, he was consciously able to demonstrate living in it. Hence, he could say, "I and the Father are One," because he lived from the place in himself that empowered him. He was in constant conscious contact with his Divinity or buddhic dimension!

As we open our lives to becoming awakened, we become more aligned to the incredible opportunity to discover our personal connection to the Christ! How is this accomplished? How is it possible to experience a personal connection to Christ in our daily lives?

All enlightened beings have suggested that we can experience a personal relationship to Christ, whether it be the Christ of Judeo-Christian thought or the buddhi of ancient India, in very definite personal ways. The process varies but the teachings are clear:

1. Study some of the sacred writings such as The Bible, The Bhagavad Gita, The Koran, The Talmud, The Upanishads, the writings of Lao-tse, with diligence, care, consistency and loving attention. Study acquaints us with age-old teachings and enables us to personally discover the Truth Principles that are still valid.

2. Develop and incorporate into our daily lives spiritual practices such as prayer, meditation, contemplation, yoga, etc. These practices enable us to slowly come to know our inner nature, to discover our own relationship to God. Thus, most importantly, we begin to feel or experience the deeper Inner Self through tapping or contacting the superconscious states of being. It is this contact and alignment which brings into our waking consciousness an awareness of the power (presence) of God within us!

3. Through the spiritual practices we release our self-imposed, limiting beliefs, attitudes or feelings that restrict, cause resistance or create inner pain. According to the ancient teacher Hermes Trismegistus, there are 12 aspects of self called "torturers" that prevent us from making our inner connection. These are: Ignorance, Grief, Incontinence, Desire, Injustice, Covetousness, Deceitfulness, Envy, Fraud, Anger, Rashness and Vice. Once we are "born again" into higher consciousness, we purify these aspects of our ego nature and move into the final state, which is ...

4. Commitment to Life through service to our fellow man. In committing to life through service to others, we take action in affirming the innate divinity in others. When we serve self-lessly (not for ego needs), we recognize that all people are incarnations of the divine. As we individually open our hearts to this, we no longer see people as separate from ourselves. We begin to actually, daily, consciously realize that each person can connect with and experience the Eternal Christ.

This Christ is the archetype, or blueprint, of the God-like, higher, truest Self in us. And yet, the Christ stands "out there", "beyond the door" of our ego, humbly seeking permission of our "nothing little self" to come in and take up His rightful abode in our body, soul and mind, to feast with us of the spiritual riches available to us all. As this acceptance occurs in our lives, we experience the heavenly kingdom and all it represents at our Father's table: Love, Joy, Peace, Forgiveness, Wisdom, Bliss, Light and Fullness of Spirit!

28

Living in the Eternal Now

"The Lord is my shepherd, I shall not want. He maketh me to lie down in green pastures; he leadeth me beside the still waters. He restoreth my soul: he leadeth me in the paths of righteousness for his name's sake."
Psalm 23:1-3

∾

Immediately that we hear or read the words "Living in the eternal now," perhaps our intellect responds with the flash thought, "Well, where else am I living, for heaven's sake?" However, the more we discover about ourselves, about our inner and outer perceptions, the more likely it is that we will learn that living in the present, i.e., staying focused in the present, can be challenging. Each of us approaches that challenge differently.

I would like to share some examples about two major areas of life that I feel might benefit from being approached from the concept of "living in the now."

In a given 24 hour period, how often do your thoughts return to activities, events and specific circumstances - be they health issues, personal or business matters - that occurred a day, several days, a week, two weeks, a month, 3 months, 6 months, a year, etc. ago? On one hand, it is useful, revealing and purposeful for each of us to evaluate, clarify and reexamine our personal past, our personal involvements and life connections to people, places and events. On the other hand, "The problem," caution teachers of the Inner Way, "is that we can become trapped in thought by our repeated returnings to experiences that are essentially over and done with, finished or finalized." If there are matters or circumstances that have not been resolved or completed and we dwell upon them in thought, we actually reenergize that condition or situation. In a larger sense, that does not serve us well. It causes us to live disconnectedly, halfheartedly and ineffectively in the present.

Conversely, attempting to live in the unknown future also creates a problematic view of life. While it can be wise, useful and highly significant to consider, reflect upon and plan for the future, the conflict or problem arises if we actively attempt to live in the future to avoid being fully present in the now. Attempting to *live* in the future will create stress, worry, anxiety and frustration. To live in the future means to desire to control people and events, to control their decisions and reactions or safeguard one's own. It is a futile effort, essentially, and a waste of precious time. It cannot be done.

For anyone to attempt to project their life, to attempt to misdirect their energies into the future will result in weakening their focus in the moment, in the now. They will lose touch with reality and their experience of themselves as human/spiritual beings. Only when such individuals can allow themselves to release future-oriented projection will they begin to act out of clarity, decision and wisdom in the here-now-present. Only by living in the eternal now can we empower ourselves to take action, resolve problems and allow ourselves to enter the Kingdom of God.

"Well," you might ask, "how is this empowerment, this living in the now accomplished?" Let us consider a somewhat abbreviated listing of ideas and practical tools which might serve as potential guidelines:

1. Start to make any necessary changes now. Make a list of circumstances needing healing, change or resolution. Next, *begin* to move, to act, to direct your energies in the direction of the change you wish to accomplish. Concentrate on one change, one thing. To attempt to change two, three or more areas or circumstances at the same time can get confusing, become overpowering and be perceived as overwhelming. Start with the simplest task and move on to the more complicated issues as you realize success and empowerment in the process.

2. If frustration should emerge, allow it; give space in your thinking and feeling nature for releasing the anxiety or frustration or fear that may surface. Say to yourself, "I can confidently and calmly release all that I fear." "God is in charge of my thought and my actions." "I give thanks." This will permit you to handle one issue at a time. Fear can polarize or paralyze. Fear can act to block even the most sincere intention to effect change. Allowing the fear discharges the energy around and about it. It permits you to free yourself to step out of the past—or the shadowy unknown aspects of the future.

3. Take God as your partner. When we truly accept that God's Presence is actually available to us, *personally*, the frightening or confusing or negative experiences of the moment fade gradually in proportion to that realization. Once having experienced that oneness, it is immensely comforting, reassuring and clarifying to know that all the *forces of the Universe* (God) are readily available to help us. Look for God everywhere, in everyone, in everything and *accept* that Presence as part of all of life's experiences. See God shining through even pain, hurt or loss. Feel God's Love supporting, healing and nurturing you in *all* circumstances. Trust God in all things and continue to move into life undeterred.

4. Do your best with your life! Let others take care of their lives! Much too often do we fear the results of others' actions or reactions and live out of a place of lack or considerable weakness. Before we can help others, we must become strong. To the best of your ability, be open and honorable to yourself—about your weaknesses and strengths. It may be important to seek professional help if you genuinely feel you need it. Seek healing or comfort as that may be appropriate. But emerge from your past... and stay focused in the now. Your future is unfolding, on time, on course, in Divine Order.

There can, of course, be challenges, perhaps even temporary "setbacks." Inner growth is seldom, if ever, a constant, even experience. However, the lesson behind it all is that to really empower ourselves, to really live in the Presence of Ultimate Reality, we must be willing to continue to do our "home work," our inner processing, while attending to our personal issues and seeing to our daily affairs. Living in the eternal now is learning how to give the most, the best and the noblest that we can offer moment by moment according to our capacity and capabilities.

To live in the now means, essentially, to truly recognize ourselves as sons and daughters of the Most High. It means to act out of wisdom with love and light and vision in all our ways and the far-reaching effects of our lives. Our every thought, word and deed moves out in a "ripple effect" to encompass the 360-degree circumference of our world. May Peace, Love and Light go forth from you into the eternal now, to return to you from the eternal now, enhanced with Life's boundless blessings.

Where we are, God is. Where God is, we are. There is One Life. That Life is God. That Life is Whole and Perfect. That Life is our life now.

29

Inner Focus/Outer Expression

"As long as we are prepared to learn, we will stay young, never aging. But the moment we say, 'I have studied and I know', we begin to grow old... The moment we let ourselves be praised as an important person, we grow old... The moment we become a teacher instead of a student, we age, time passes, intelligence disappears, and we are left to face our Judgment Day."

M. R. Bawa Muhaiyaddeen

∾

Life affords change, challenge and constant opportunity to draw from the chalice of our being that which allows us to deepen, broaden, and grow more conscious. Yet the pull of the ego, the personality and the material, human dimension often causes us to forget that the work of enlightenment is one of remembering who we really are.

To *remember* suggests a conscious recalling, a returning to what was known, experienced or otherwise perceived. On the physical level, our brain cells - in fact, all cells of the human flesh body—have a certain, very distinct biological memory. If this "automatic" memory failed, we would never grow or mature, nor would we be able to operate (function) as human beings. At deeper levels of our nature, *remembering* occurs when we yearn to express a specific skill or talent, such as painting, sketching, singing, or any form of art, or to reveal a knowledge such as an esoteric truth, or bring forth an invention, or teach a spiritual process. It is not only the yearning or inclination as such that signals a memory, but the *knowledge* that we have either accomplished it before, such as in some former life pattern, or that we bring with us the inner capacity to perform, develop and express that yearning, that deep soul urge to reveal the highest qualities attendant to such a powerful desire.

Deliberately, consciously and with deep intention then, learning as much as we can about our true self or making a special effort to gain understanding of what we are and how we ultimately function in the world, is what brings forth our wisdom and eventually our own Spiritual Destiny.

Remembering is an inner reclaiming and refining of our most sacred, holy, and unfolding self. It is the gradual and ultimate full joy of knowing and discovering that we are awakening to Life's Impulse, to the Demi-Urge to the very power of God.

Living day to day, if we do not remain centered, we lose our deep spiritual clarity and inner focus. Human needs, mundane affairs, ego demands, mental preoccupations and ideas cloud our real vision, our sense of inner direction and purpose. It is at times like these that we must affirm the I AM Presence through spiritual practices such as prayer, meditation, affirmation, attendance at church or involvement with useful and purposeful projects dedicated to uplift, inspire and transform us and the planet upon which we live.

Roy Eugene Davis writes that, "...the more we allow the Divine Force to flow through mind and body, the more radiant will mind and body become. You will also notice that other people are uplifted when they are in your presence, and when you think of them or they think of you."

The unfolding of our real nature must occur in and through our life, as our life. It is not separate from our daily activities. Go about your daily activities focused with your mind centered on God. Josephine Whitney Duveneck writing in *Fellowship In Prayer* (Vol. 36, No. 2), says, "Before entering anyone's doorway, I made a practice of inaudibly invoking a blessing upon the house. This was an old Hebrew custom and interestingly enough, I found it still carried on among the simple folk of Ireland. When joining a group or meeting an individual, I thought 'May God accompany me'. At the beginning of a committee and during the course of discussion I tried to imagine God was there among us as an invisible, but somehow participating extra entity, not an embodiment but an essence - an unsubstantiated presence that could ease tensions and flow into decisions and assure the moral justification of compromises... at first this seemed a bothersome, idiotic obligation, but gradually the effort subsided into habit. My patience expanded with practice."

The outer expression of our life is but a gradual awakening to what is within us. "He who opens the rose, does it so simply", wrote Tagore. In the physical arena, the natural world, we get distracted by our encumbrances, our diversions, our fragmented emotions, wants, and wishes. Willy Yaryan writing in "The Householder and the Pilgrim" (*Fellowship In Prayer*, Vol. 36, No. 2), says it profoundly and simply: "God is Presence, and there are thousands of reasons to forget. The trial, in all its forms, is to remember; to remember to say grace before taking the first mouthful of food, to remember to forgive everyone everything before drifting off to sleep, to remember that life, no matter how trivial or dramatic is holy."

The conscious act of remembering, then, is a silent, subtle call from the deepest, innermost dimensions of our being to allow what we know and understand of our life experience to become our own! It is the constant, consistent acknowledgment that God's Presence is everywhere, always flowing, functioning and unfolding in, through and as our life, day to day, moment by precious moment. Such knowledge invites us to continue our journey, to really permit the tasks of the day to be what they are, great or small, trivial or important, and to accept that our awakening is occurring from the tiniest, most infinitesimal units of cellular life to our ever expanding and deepening consciousness.

30

Understanding the Divine Spirit Within Us

"Trust in the Lord, and do good; so will you dwell in the land and enjoy security. Take delight in the Lord, and he will give you the desires of your heart."
Psalm 37:3,4

∾

One of the very basic qualities needed for living an effective, dynamic and contented life is trust. Yet skeptics and secular cynics often suggest that trust is the hallmark of the gullible. In a study reported by *Psychology Today* magazine, the work of Dr. Julian Rotter from the University of Connecticut revealed some fascinating clues about the nature of trust and the consequences of its influence on human behavior and personality development. In essence, he discovered that the trusting person is healthy; the untrusting person is unhealthy. Trusting people are *less gullible* than non-trusting persons! Trusting people are less susceptible to a rip-off artist than are non-trusting people! Yet, even in the face of such evidence, the human race tends to feel negative, fearful, resentful, anxious, guilty and inferior overall.

The various sacred traditions and teachings all concur in the theology, the idea, that our Divine Nature is accessible to us, that it is ever available to us to use for our development. However, there are many and diverse ways to approach getting in contact with and accessing the dormant power awaiting our awakening. Capturing and embracing the Divine Spark (Spirit) is not so much an intellectual mental process as it is a soul recognition of how our Divine Essence is triggered and how it emerges and manifests in the patterns of our lives.

The concept of developing trust has been suggested as a means to help experience an effective, dynamic and contented life. As a means of helping us to move beyond the limitations of directing our lives from the focus of negative emotions, such as resentment, fear, anxiety and guilt about ourselves or others, let us examine the proposition of developing trust in our waking, day to day affairs and relationships and using that as a springboard to explore our Divine Potential.

The following questionnaire may serve as a guideline to help answer whether or not you are at this moment ready, willing and receptive to the idea of moving ahead, *trusting* in your greater good. Do not deliberate your responses. Your first impression is your basic, honest answer. There are 10 questions and the answers you give will assist you to measure whether you are a *possibility person*, or whether you may need to reconsider your present lifestyle strategy. One last thought before you begin. There are no *right* or *wrong* answers. There are just *different* answers, indicative of different places in mind concepts and individual understandings.

1. Do you look for reasons why something can't be done instead of searching for ways in which it can be done?
2. Do you ever make major or minor decisions based on fear of the outcome?
3. Do you tend to resist new ideas and prefer to do things the way you've always done them?
4. Do you move ahead only after you've gathered together every single fact?
5. Do you have the tendency to demand a guarantee of success before you begin?
6. Do you imagine opposition you will encounter (to your ideas of a project) rather than the support you hope for or might expect?
7. Do you ever turn down an idea simply because you "don't like it"?
8. Do you close your mind to suggestions even before hearing the full explanations?
9. Do you point out what you consider the disadvantages of an idea before you point out the advantages?
10. Do you ever make negative decisions because you're tired or because it seems easier to do so?

If you answered 8 or more of the questions in the affirmative, you may want to consider getting a spiritual prescription from your nearest minister or teacher. You could be finding life pretty uncomfortable right now.

If your score was 5 or more in the affirmative, you're beginning to be a risk taker. Please continue and see how many possibilities open up to you.

If you answered 3 or more affirmatively, you've taken the leap of faith and aren't afraid to try and trust and trust again!

A score of 1 or 2 in the affirmative probably means that you've made significant inroads into your spiritual quest and inner journey and *know* that in order to explore *any* part of life, one must be open, vulnerable to the moment, and willing to trust the universe in all things! Give thanks and continue!

The nature of life is to unfold, to grow and to change. We see consistent evidence of this as we examine our own personal process from childhood into adulthood. The whole experience of growth suggests that where and what we are at any given moment cannot have depth or meaning or give us strength unless we are willing to accept that God does indeed have a place at the very center of our being!

There can be no real trust in life's goodness unless we eliminate resentment, guilt, fear and anxiety. Understanding the Divine spirit within us is accepting, through grace, the mystery of God's Loving Presence as ours! Repeatedly, God tells us that we are his children, that we are sons and daughters of the Living God, that we are made in His Image! While our intellect and our rational mind may struggle to accept that promise, the truth will undergird and benefit our lives clearly and unmistakably. As we accept that we are made in the Image and Likeness of God, we become aware of our possibilities, our potentials, our capabilities! When we are focused upon our limitations or what isn't working, or what is blocking our progress, or what is causing us to feel trapped, our Divine Nature gets set aside. We choose right there what path we will take. Be like Joshua of the Old Testament who stated, "As for me and my house, we will serve the Lord."

To serve the Lord is not a vague scriptural injunction. It is the providential acknowledgment of our Holy Connection, our Divine Flame, our Sacred Spark! Trust, as an action in our life, is a major step in building self esteem, creating new opportunities, resolving problems, healing hurts and allowing ourselves to be really open to the promise "With God all things are possible," "I can do all things through Christ who strengthens me."

31

Acres of Diamonds

"And God saw everything that he had made, and behold, it was very good." **Genesis 1:31**

"Earth's crammed with heaven, and every common bush afire with God." **Elizabeth Barrett Browning**

∾

A diamond is defined as being a pure or nearly pure form of carbon, crystallized, in the isometric system, of extreme hardness and when used as a precious stone, of great brilliance. (American College Dictionary)

Special images quickly flood the mind screen when the word "diamond" is spoken. From pictures of bejeweled crowns and elegant jewelry to stories concerning world famous stones such as the Hope Diamond, they suggest and evoke images of great wealth, power and prestige.

However, in their natural state, diamonds are unpretentious and "insignificant", appearing to the naked eye as cloudy, relatively small, somewhat rounded greasy stones. No one who is unfamiliar with them in their natural state would spot the Silent Stone and recognize it for its inherent value.

It is only after they have been mined and separated into the four major varieties, (1) diamond proper, (2) bort, (3) ballas, and (4) carbonado, and then categorized as either gem or industrial quality, weighed, divided (cleaved) and ultimately polished that they take on the values ascribed to them by gemologists, jewelers, industrialists, etc.

There are a number of approaches to cleaving or dividing the natural stones and the color varies from colorless to black and they may be transparent, translucent or opaque. Most diamonds used as gemstones are transparent and colorless, or nearly so.

Each of us in our initial spiritual perceptions of ourselves or others are somewhat like the uncut, unpolished, rough stone diamonds. With our varied shapes and sizes, our particular personal appearances, our emotional makeup, tastes and preferences can be all but invisible to others. We hide or block or choose not to see the reality and beauty of our true nature, our sacred self.

Often it is not until we begin the careful and somewhat tedious work of sorting out and "cutting away and polishing" (refining) that we discover who we really are. We look at the outside and see roughness, cloudiness, heaviness or darkness. We do much the same with others. We see their "unpolished" appearance, their lack of education, refinement or sensitivity—and reject them as being of no value; i.e., unfit, undeserving or unacceptable.

We can learn much about ourselves (and others) from understanding something of the process of "transformation" that the diamond, the hardest natural substance known to man, passes through on its way to becoming a jewel, the setting for a brooch, the focus of a wedding ring, necklace or kingly crown.

All around us, life offers gifts. The sensitive soul sees the spirit, the vision, the potential and possibility of life's experiences. Those of limited vision cast away the gift as straw or rubble, as dirt or dung.

Conflicts or problems sometimes initially appear as uncut diamonds—their unseemliness hide or disguise the finer gifts they would reveal. We must be patient in the sorting, refining and polishing process if we would discover the opportunities that the conflicts or problems conceal.

Perhaps the most difficult challenge in our lives is to accept the possibility that *all* of our experiences ... especially the confusing, painful and frightening ones—have value and significance. Most people can readily accept good fortune, favorable conditions and positive responses to personal encounters. It is something else to even consider that there might be a "hidden beauty" (positive outcome) in an accident resulting in physical crippling, scarring or disfiguring. This requires a stretch beyond the appearances to see the possibility of a purpose or plan, or that any inner wisdom exists. It demands a profound process to discern the hidden clarity which awaits the person who experiences bankruptcy or foreclosure, for example, or who is victimized through the deliberate dishonesty of others.

Love is still available after one has lost a spouse, a friend or a partner. One can find peace beneath the surface of conditions or situations causing anxiety, frustration, or even depression. It requires the individual thus afflicted to first accept and then learn in gradual, delicate increments that Life is waiting to heal, to bless, honor, uplift and to nurture!

Shifting an attitude, forgiving one's self or another, breaking a restrictive or limiting pattern awaits our decision. The real gift awaits our being willing to see through the limitation, look beyond the appearance to the deeper truth, to the inner beauty that calls.

Our lives contain Acres of Diamonds near at hand. They are in our homes, our jobs, our businesses, our churches. Search, if need be, in the hearts of others, search in the avenues and byways of life. Diamonds are found both in the experience of the search and in the *process* of the discovery.

Dr. Russell H. Conwell, past President of Temple University, first delivered his lecture "Acres of Diamonds" before the Yale College of Law in 1921. He repeated the lecture over 4,000 times throughout America and abroad and is reputed to have earned well over $1,000,000 from it. His ideas have a familiar ring as we read his words, "You don't need to go out of your house to find where the diamonds are. You don't need to go out of your own room. Sit there in the quiet or, in bed, lie there - *with an open mind to sense things, a soul open to inspiration. There are things for you to do, there are Acres of Diamonds for you, closer than you dream of.*"

32

The Creative Power of Love

"A new commandment I give unto you, that you love one another; as I have loved you, that ye also love one to another. By this shall all men know that ye are my disciples, if ye have love one to another." **John 13:34,35**

∾

In attempting to understand our experience of Love (Life), we often try to explain, theorize and intellectualize with our limited human consciousness: "what God is doing" in our lives. How can we possibly know which circumstances are going to work out for our greater good—or which people are going to be *best* for us? Yet, when we are in the flow of Love (Life), we can learn by being open, or receptive, to life—knowing that God nourishes us through all expressions of Himself; i.e., through all people and in every situation and circumstance. In truth, God is present, motivating and directing our lives in specific and powerful ways. We can say with the poets, *God works in strange and mysterious ways His wonders to perform.*

The real work of love in our lives is done daily. It's the attitude we have about our job, career or task at hand that determines the values or meaning and benefit of it. There may be financial goals or ambitions, social, personal or other objectives, but if we are open or receptive to *process* each experience in the moment, we can realize what the flow of life is truly gifting or revealing to us.

Hence the Biblical adage, "Give and it shall be given unto you..." suggests that *we* regulate the flow of God's abundance or goodness and opportunities in our lives. If we give out harshness, we reap harshness; if we express hurt, bitterness, judgment, we open ourselves to receive pain, hurt, bitterness and judgment. On the other hand, if we send out love, joy and gratitude, then we become receptive to love, joy and gratitude.

It behooves us to learn to give deep, inner, profound thanks for whatever we have at the present moment in our lives. This is what we have to work with. Do not deny circumstances or conditions. Do not "stew" about them. Face each aspect or situation with love, patience and forbearance. According to our individual ability to move into the flow of Love (Life), we become open to new opportunities, people and changing life circumstances that offer us our greater good. Thus, *if we can accept* what God has already shown (given) us through our talents (potentials, skills, capabilities), we open ourselves to become very powerfully and profoundly inspired by God's Activity in (and through and as) us.

In order to become more completely open and receptive to the activity of love in our lives, wherever we desire it, we must begin by loving (accepting God's Presence in) ourselves. This step is called opening to the Source. Prayer stimulates us to do this. Meditation enables us to touch our transcendent self and know, in a more direct way, the real connection we seek. Whenever we begin to feel any kind of connectedness to the Source, we then slowly enter a second phase in our unfoldment called release.

Releasing any past pains, hurts, feelings and related conditional aspects of love will allow us to see a bigger picture, a greater plan—a more radiant set of possibilities. However, as long as we say to ourselves, "I'll never forget or forgive my former friend (or spouse, parent or child, employer or coworker) for the way they treated me," we literally continue to create with our thought energies the same patterns, situations and conflicts in our lives. Sometimes we hold onto the past deliberately, with full knowledge of what we're doing. Consciously and continually reviewing our hurts, slights and woundednesses. Sometimes we do this unknowingly or unconsciously. The results are the same. All spiritual teachers and truth teachings agree on this point: the past is over. We need to place it into perspective, bless it, give it whatever is appropriate acknowledgment and move on!

A final step (for the sake of this discussion) of being creatively in the flow of Love (Life) thus emerges. We must choose to take the responsibility to live fully in the now. It is not enough to pray or to meditate. It is not enough to enter levels of higher consciousness or expanded awareness. It is not enough to passively accept God's Loving Presence or to make partial or token efforts to release the past. It is necessary that we take personal responsibility for our lives. It is necessary that we try to help make the world (the people around us as well as the larger community) in which we live a better place.

And how is this accomplished? Through service to life. Service to others, to the church, school, community or environment in which we share our lives. The active demonstration of love becomes truly creative when we support a larger vision, a greater ideal, a higher purpose beyond our personal lives. There are thousands of worthwhile projects, noble causes and inspired and dedicated people whose work is purposeful, useful and spiritually valuable that we may relate to or align ourselves with. Our growth objective is service to humanity within our abilities, capacities of time and the structure and patterns of our individual lives.

Ultimately, we must find and identify our own form of service. Robert Schuller, pastor of the world famous Crystal Cathedral in California, says, "Find a need and fill it, find a heart and heal it...". When we are tempted to stray into useless pursuits and involvements, our deep inner promptings - the flow of Love (Life) energies - will bring us back on course to what is important. Roy Eugene Davis writes in his *Open Your Life to Infinite Good*, "The world about us is the result of past causes. Introduce new causes and learn to see clearly the available good before you. In this manner you will learn to live as a free being as you were designed to live."

It is in being receptive to life that we can be creative. The more we open to express, to give, to share, to demonstrate, the more life opens, gives, expresses to us. Love, then, is an activity of our God nature seeking ever to express itself in myriad forms through our life.

33

A Time for New Beginnings

Upon the journey of our individual lives, the young, the old, the wise, the foolish, the spiritually awakened and those yet unaware, the eternal question of ancient and modern seeker alike is queried, "Can we begin anew?"

From the most illumined writings of the saints, sages and holy men many thousands of years old to the most recent findings of modern mind/brain research and the very latest discoveries of human genetics, nuclear as well as psychosomatic medicine, ample evidence is accumulating that we are not limited to our old concepts, outworn attitudes, restrictive bodies or physical emotional, mental and psychological impairments.

Jean Houston, author, teacher, educator and psychologist extraordinaire, in *The Possible Human*, suggests that internal images, feelings and energy systems known to the ancients and now modern man can amplify and change the entire direction of our life. She suggests serious meditation practices as one way to accomplish this.

W. Brugh Joy, M.D., author of *Joy's Way*, (a significant book on the nature of the transformative process) has for the past several years directed and facilitated weekend and week long "deepenings"—experiential retreat environments that provide major shifts that awaken dormant potential and bring life changing movement to those who truly participate and allow themselves to be receptive to the experience.

Joseph Chilton Pearce, author, scientist, educator, a brilliant scholar (*Crack in the Cosmic Egg*), articulates that man has hardly awakened to his sleeping potential, but once stirred can become the source of enormous change and positive redirection in the world affecting literally everything and everyone in the universe.

In experiencing movies like *Resurrection* (starring Ellen Burstyn) with its incredible theme of healing, to *E.T., the Extra-Terrestrial* whose touch healed, transformed and awakened much of America and the world to the possibilities of love and acceptance of "alien" forms, to *Gandhi* (Ben Kingsley) whose life was not in vain in his affirmation for peace, to *Yentl* (starring Barbra Streisand) in which we are reminded that sexuality does not have preference in God's Kingdom for the rights of learning, growing or becoming who we are, we are clearly shown that life is ever renewing itself across the world, across the face of time in countless ways and forms.

A Course In Miracles, a series of three books published by The Foundation of Inner Peace, suggests that we are governed principally by either fear or love (peace) and that the way to inner peace is the overcoming of the way of hurt, loss, anger, fear and death. And further, that living moment by moment in the conscious awareness of real peace—an accessible, tangible inner state that harmonizes with all life and allows us a transformative view of life—can bring daily renewal and quicken us with the eternal pulse of the flow of the universe.

The essential ingredient, from sage to scientist alike, necessary for beginning anew is actually accepting inwardly at the very deepest level of our being that change is indeed possible, desirable and viable. Motivational psychologists, human potential teachers, ministers, leaders and spiritual teachers alike around the globe agree that at some deep inner level of our being we actually initiate the movement that manifests in our outer life as changed consciousness, a new attitude, a different perspective, a more whole view that our life, our experience of our reality, our personal existence can be different, better, richer, fuller, deeper and more abundant.

The journey from acceptance to the experience of the actual change we desire is called *awakening, enlightenment, transformation, renewal, rebirth* ; in short, *spiritual growth*.. The struggle to overcome, release our old habits, fears and patterns and create vital new directions and goals on any level of our complex being is not only possible but the necessary movement of our life to becoming ultimately the enlightened, the awakened and God conscious individual we are potentially!

Let us joyously respond to Life's invitation to grow, deepen, broaden and awaken to our unfolding rose, The Thousand Petaled Lotus of eastern thought—to The Spiral of God—The Ladder of Lights—The Christ Presence—The Light, The Source—The God Within!

34

The Mystical Marriage of Spirit

> ***"Not merely reflecting but manifesting the Spiritual Light, man rises to the awareness of the kingdom of God. There he abandons the idea of separate existence and attains full release and oneness with Spirit."***
>
> **Veda - Hindu Scripture**

∾

The old adage, "The proof of the pudding is in the eating," applies as much today as when it was first originated. In every area of life, from our physical world to our sense of the larger spiritual reality, we are called upon to demonstrate, or to make real our beliefs. Thus it is that we must individually learn how to prove the principles of universal truth, for—*"What does it profit, my brethren, though a man say he hath faith, and have not works? Can faith save him?...For as the body without the spirit is dead, so faith without works is dead also."* (James 2:14 and 16)

In a spiritual sense, the mystical marriage is the process and realization of the already existing union of the deepest, known and unknown forces within us to that Source which we call Ultimate Cause, Ultimate Reality, Divine Mind—God!

In a social sense, marriage is defined as a union of a legal nature between a man and a woman. Connotatively, marriage suggests the possibility of a growing, evolving, deepening relationship—a unique strengthening or blending of inner forces—a sacred connecting of opposite energies sometimes psychologically labeled as "masculine" and "feminine" Marriage is also the *form* of the relationship with a spouse. For example, we agree to live in the same environment (house or apartment), to raise a family (or not to do so), to work together, to play or create together, however that is mutually and individually defined. Thus we might say, a marriage is a relationship of two individuals who seek ideally to blend those same deepest, known and unknown forces within to bring about the actual experience of the inner and outer marriage, union, connection. Let's discuss some ideas or aspects about relationships that might help give us some clarity.

When we are "attracted" to someone, that attraction most often is a recognition of feelings within ourselves that we hope, or indeed tend to discover as mutually existent in that other person. We then progress successively from recognizing that attraction and feeling as sensual, sexual, emotional, mental, psychological or spiritual. Depending upon a host of circumstances—such as perhaps feeling confident, the attraction being socially acceptable, or rightly motivated—we **act** upon our feelings or perceptions and move toward the development of a friendship or relationship. We begin to express ourselves toward that association.

Whether the attraction is purely friendship or for a more intimate relationship, nothing will come of it if it isn't mutual. If any or some or all of the above circumstances, and forces and facets of our inner nature are acceptable, then a relationship is possible. A gradual blending or uniting of energies develops *within* us *and between* us. This blending gradually expands or progresses. It can then be said that a relationship between the inner and the outer exists—a "mystical marriage" is said to then exist. Let it also be said that we have many acquaintanceship, but very few deep friendships in our lives. In that mystical relationship, our lover, sweetheart, or spouse is, or should be, also our best friend. With a Friend as with a Mate, a mystical union occurs when we mutually give it our very best. Only then will our faith, trust and belief translate into works, trust, productivity!

We have this moment, now! We string our lives together, moment by moment in the forever now. Whatever the circumstances of our life, we have the power to mold it and change it as we will by the mystical marriage of our mind with our spirit. Perhaps you are dealing with the aftermath of a loved one's death. Maybe you are facing a health challenge, or job loss or change. Are you or someone you know or love emotionally troubled? Whatever our lot in this moment now, we need to remind ourselves each one that there is a Profound Presence that supports our being, our process, our acting upon or following through with what we need to make our life more complete.

When we consider the Biblical commandment to love our neighbor as ourselves, we are reminded that loving begins with us first. We are in our physical forms. We are here in time-space on planet earth. Life isn't something that's waiting to happen. Life is in process in this moment, now! So love, then, is already ours. Love calls to us in its myriad forms (including loving our actual next-door neighbors) to be accepted, embraced and experienced.

The opportunity to mold or change our life is experienced in a similar manner. It is already here! The mystical marriage occurs (the union of attractions and/or opposites) when we act on, respond to or develop what is presented to us. If we are given an invitation to visit a museum, to see a play, try a new (different) restaurant, attempt a new job, develop or begin to master a new skill or talent, or whatever—*and we accept*, a mystical marriage occurs. All of the hidden and unseen forces of the universe await to aid us! In religious language, we call this "Waiting on God." As we begin to move in the direction of the opportunity, a connection is made, development and expansion are realized. We are not "locked in" to defeat, limitation, hurt or pain. We must seize the opportunity of the NOW, to take all that which God gave us and mold it nearer to our heart's desire!

So it is with living the Spiritual Life. A mystical union or linkage occurs when we begin to *apply* what we study. Many seekers study assiduously. They attend one class after another, workshop upon workshop, conference after conference. It seems to be "a game of mental gymnastics." They keep juggling or balancing more knowledge, more information, but it seems they fail to put much of it into practice. Their attention is diverted with reading the latest New Thought or metaphysical book, studying the "newest" technique or workshop promising "total transformation". The point is obvious. Living the spiritual life is just that! It's in the doing! It's a *daily* effort to live the ideal life as best we understand what that means, to the best of our abilities. Living the spiritual life requires of us a profound willingness to incorporate (blend) into our lives what we individually know we must do.

Roy Eugene Davis writes of this in *Open Your Life to Infinite Good*, "Whatever are your talents and abilities, whatever you have to share with your world, find some way to intelligently do so. This is the most direct approach to working in harmony with God's will on earth. Attend to your duties with a cheerful heart, knowing that all you do is important to the total process... Yearn for the awareness of God all the time, even while involved in routine matters. Do not separate the material, social and spiritual aspects of your life. Let God be with you in all that you do... Be a conscious and willing representative of God in this world. Whatever you have to use and share wisely, do so. You will find that more is made available to you. You cannot exhaust the treasure house of the universe because the source of all that is, is God."

35

Enhancement of the Spirit of God Within Us

As we journey upon the spiritual quest, each of us is confronted by a series of worldly distractions, previous conditionings, emotional, mental and psychological conflicts, attachments and all manner of ego experiences that interfere with the discovery of the "God Nature Within". The Question is asked over and over, "Are these confusing and disturbing experiences really necessary in the process of awakening to the Inner Self?"

Each of us enters into the conscious discovery of our Divine Nature at a different point along our life's path. One may come to recognize the perimeters of the innate sacred nature of life through personal grief or loss of a loved one. Another may approach the inner self through psychic revelation or experiences such as precognition, dreams or some other kind of psychic manifestation. Personal crisis such as divorce, destruction of property through fire, flood or other natural catastrophe creates the resonance that triggers a search for deeper meaning. Still others have a near brush with death, such as cancer, heart attack or stroke, during which periods, as they recover or eventually make their transition, they reach out to become open to or awakened to the essence of their deepest or Divine Nature.

In each of these instances, and in a myriad variety of other ways, the call of the Demi-urge, or that part of our greatest yearning, our Sacred, Divine Beingness, is gently beckoning to us. Thus, our age, sex, intelligence, occupation, station in life, moral or ethical behavior as far a society is concerned, has essentially no bearing upon when we begin to respond to the Inner Voice or what happens when we hear it.

Once the Inner Voice, that which is sometimes called the intuition, (or the Still Small Voice) begins to manifest in our life, there are many significant ways to enhance the Spirit of God within us.

1. **Honor, own, pay attention to your own life's statement** to you about what's happening to you. Don't discount, discredit or deny the reflecting mirror of your personal reality. It is the substance, the modeling clay of your growth and learning.

2. **Be willing to accept yourself** as you are and others as they are. Comparing yourself to others may be helpful to gain a sense of perspective, but most often it leads to self-criticism, self-judgment and other self-defeating behavior.

3. **Surrender false ego values**, personality issues, mental and emotional attachments and replace them with self acceptance, personal esteem, integrity and positive images relating to your spiritual beingness.

4. **Support life in all its richness** and variety by connecting consciously with it. Participate in life by playing, working, cooperating, relaxing and entering into life's panoramic vista wherever you are. You do not need to be a part of "special" groups or be near "spiritually awakened" teachers in order to realize your Inner Divine Nature. Since we are already Divine, in essence, all we must do is to become conscious of our connection by doing something to activate, stimulate or otherwise encourage our "sleeping self" to awaken and experience the Inner Light.

5. **The practice of certain disciplines** such as prayer, yoga, meditation and study of sacred writings will give clarity to the seeker. Disciplines do not enlighten mankind ... they purify the mental and emotional vehicles so that the Inner Light may shine through us more clearly

Enhancement of the Spirit of God Within is accessible on a daily basis, *wherever* we are, *whatever* we are doing with our personal lives. It is significant to remember that we are never apart from or separate from God. It is only when we deny the God Within through doubt, fear, anger, resentment or any other kind of negative state that we limit our good or block our greater unfoldment.

To nurture, sustain and develop a consciousness that encourages and enhances the Spirit of God In Us, the following affirmation is suggested as a positive way to acknowledge our inner spark: *"From the Depths of my being I joyously respond to Life's Invitation to Grow, Unfold, and to Experience Completion and all Life's Infinite Good!"*

36

New Beginnings - One Step At A Time

"For everyone that asketh receiveth; and he that seeketh findeth; and to him that knocketh it shall be opened." **St. Matthew 7:8**

∾

To be born into physical life, to have taken on incarnation of flesh and blood signifies that we have chosen an opportunity to learn more about who we are. Learning about ourselves physically, mentally, spiritually and emotionally consumes the totality of our life. In fact, it becomes the major or real and total reason for our existence.

If it is true that we choose our individual life experience—our parents, family, environment and all else associated with our personal circumstances—as many, many enlightened teachers have suggested and/or revealed, why is it that we struggle so with our personal life, our day to day living, our relationships with our mates, children, family, friends, social, business and religious worlds? Why do we resist learning from the actual direct confrontations or occasions of inharmony? or loss? or grief? or deep frustration, depression or anger?

Humanity, it seems, has a love affair with winners: all the world loves a winner. Literature, theater, movies, sports and entire magazines abound with stories and the accomplishments of winners who succeeded against insurmountable odds. Something in us is lifted, inspired and thrilled by our own or the victories of others!

Struggling implies a process called work, dealing with obstacles, overcoming problems. Starting over, a step at a time, is perceived at the start of retracing our steps as being incompatible with the end result of victory. We can relate, individually, to the attainments of a great hero and join in the jubilant triumph of the athlete as he or she achieves Olympic stature and honor. We are inspired by the person who manages to work a "miracle" against a health affliction, or by the stalwart who overcomes great odds in life to win a battle in court, victory over an oppressor in the workplace, or a reconciliation between feuding partners, family members or friends. We are buoyed by their demonstration of the special skills, talents or capabilities called forth in the course of their attainment. Yet our own struggle is often too great or too painful and, therefore, it is easier to hide behind the mask of failure than to try to make the effort to change. We miss the opportunity to grow and learn from our lessons and thus we put off our own good. We delay our own success.

Psychologists, therapists, medical people and spiritual teachers alike agree that any successful demonstration of a goal resolution comes through *process*, the step by step effort we make to gain our objectives. Resistance is a form of denial, a tendency to not see, sense, feel, or otherwise be aware of what we individually are experiencing as hurt, disappointment, loss or futility. If we focus only upon what we want to see or experience and not what our life is revealing to us, we become trapped and caught in our problem(s) or difficulty(ies). It is that denial which must be overcome, healed and released.

Beginning anew suggests rethinking and making renewed effort. It means asking for help one more time even when it appears that every available source of help is closed off to us! It is trusting and learning discernment that permits us to explore a different possibility for change.

A close friend of mine, upon being told that she had less then six months to live with an inoperable brain tumor (cancerous), exploded angrily at her doctor and told him that her time had not yet come! She went home and after much thought, totally revised her life priorities. She began to pray. She gradually became less resentful. She changed her diet completely and began to live her life as fully each day as she could find ways to do it. She developed meditational practices. She began to visualize healing energies flowing through her bloodstream, especially through the upper part of her body and her brain. She literally, a step at a time, began her life anew. It took great courage for her to join Alcoholics Anonymous to assist the healing of her problem with alcohol. She found strength to forgive the husband who deserted her when their third child was only three months old. She truly resolved not to hide from her pain or her hurt.

Her brain tumor stopped growing. It began to shrink! She continued her regimen and the tumor got smaller and smaller. Eventually it no longer showed up at all on x-ray or on any other medical examination. Her (bewildered) doctor released her. That was six years ago and she is still well and whole. She has remarried and is happily raising her family. She has also returned to college and is working on her degree in art education.

Beginning anew means asking to be led in *the paths of righteousness* and then doing what we can to move in the direction of the assistance we are expecting. The subtle message is that we ask! The great teachers have all shared their wisdom and all have said in a variety of ways—that we must ask. In asking, humbly and prayerfully, we enter the state of *trust*, knowing that the prayer, the request will be filled and that we must then accept (receive) our good. This is the finding or discovery aspect. As we open to life's message, its bounty, its brilliance and its opportunity, we discover that our needs are filled.

Each of us must come to discover that winning is possible for us in our lives. It doesn't mean that we must become tycoons or multimillionaires, or that we must aspire to or achieve fame, honor or great position necessarily. We win when we realize that we are in charge of our personal affairs, our personal circumstances, our daily activities. We can be victorious when we mobilize all of our abilities and learn to utilize our weaknesses or our resistances (also called our negative thoughts), our fears or our previous sense or experiences of loss, futility or failure.

Beginning anew does not mean to return to ground (grade) level zero, or to the very beginning. It does mean, however, to be able to be courageous, strong and determined *to continue* to do each thing that comes before us. It is the capacity to fully trust God as our Invisible Partner and to go forth as fully aware of the Infinite Presence in every area and arena in our lives knowing that help, assistance and guidance is ours...daily.

Tom Johnson, minister of the West Valley Church of Religious Science in Canoga Park, California has written a book titled *You Are Always Your Own Experience*. The title really states the message of the book and is essentially what is implied here. We are responsible for and, knowingly and unknowingly, create our own life experience! The more we begin to truly activate the deep forces for great good that reside within our lives, the more we awaken and deepen our spiritual nature and become more fully conscious of who we are.

No more shall I look to the far skies for my
Father's loving aid;
Since here upon earth His treasure lies, and
here is His kingdom laid.
No more through the mist of things unknown I'll
search for the Promised Land;
For time is the footstool of His throne, and I am
within His hand.
The wealth that is more than finest gold is here,
if I shall but ask;
And wisdom unguessed and power untold are
here for every task.
The gates of heaven are before my eyes;
Their key is within my hand;
No more shall I look to the far skies;
For here is the Promised Land.

Alva Romanes
(*Working With the Law*
by Raymond Holliwell)

37

God's Love, Eternal Creation

"Surrounding me is all of the life that God created in His Love. It calls to me in every heartbeat and in every breath; in every action and in every thought. Peace fills my heart, and floods my body with the purpose of forgiveness... Each heartbeat brings me peace, each breath infuses me with strength. I am a messenger of God, directed by His Voice, sustained by Him in love, and held forever quiet and at peace within His loving Arms."

"Choose Once Again"
selections from *A Course in Miracles*

∾

Imagine living in a universe in which we are infused with, embraced and totally nurtured by an ever-present, all-caring, all-encompassing gentle, holy, healing, force. Of such is the very essence or character of what we know and call God's Love. It is beyond all description in words or metaphor; incapable of being understood by the intellect or measured by science. It moves beyond man's effort to contain, control or know it. Yet, it is somehow the very essence of our nature, the vibrating, pulsating rhythm of our inner life that enables us to become, ultimately, who and what we are.

Often, as we experience our life day by day, the routine and the challenge of living in the mundane world, we can and do lose sight of a sense of connectedness to the Source of our being. We move from a place of awareness of the larger universe and the nurturing embrace of God's Loving Presence, into fear, hurt, concerns over problems, ego issues, personality constraints and other distractions of the material world, the so-often referred to "human dimension". When this shift of focus occurs, we over-identify with our human frailties or weaknesses. As this happens, in the Biblical sense, we "fall from grace". The result is that during that time, or period of apparent or seeming loss, we experience the darkness, the pain of separation from Source, the sense that Love is gone or not available or not possible.

Within all of the New Thought movement, regardless of its many forms or labels, agreement exists as to the principle that underlies New Thought philosophy. Specifically, the one idea that prevails is this: Man is capable of changing his life by changing his thoughts about himself, his environment, his milieu, his world. That knowledge, while not new in the total sense, provides us with the option that our life is not confined, constricted or limited; that we can experience a new creation of our life and its accompanying circumstances by changing our attitude, our thoughts and our perceptions about our world.

God's love, as an aspect of the Eternal Creative force of the Universe, flows unto us to mend broken human relationships and to heal our physical, emotional and mental challenges, great or small. It comforts, heals and sustains us regardless of outer appearances. All that is required of us is that we accept, become open to, receptive to, aligned with, attuned to the loving Power and Presence in the Universe. Dr. Rocco Errico, famed teacher of the Aramaic translation of the Bible, writes in *New Thought Magazine*, ("Bible Basics"), "Just think of it - a universe filled with the dynamic energies of love! Since we are all children of the cosmos, our very own beings are filled with the...power of love. When we live in love, we are expressing the very warm, creative power or intelligence we call God."

When our life is "in the flow" or "on course" it is relatively easy to live and accept the experience of God's Love being ours by right of consciousness. It is when sudden death of a precious loved one happens, or illness strikes, or serious problematic issues occur that we need to consciously—through one of many spiritual practices available such as prayer, meditation, use of mantras, or yogic disciplines—remind ourselves again of our ultimate connection to the healing, nurturing all loving Source.

Our Lord taught us that in order to love, we must begin with ourselves, by forgiving ourselves and others, by releasing our past, our problems and our fears. As we realize that, love begins, as a seed energy in us and radiates outward in word and deed; it is only then that we come to grips with the potential of love within us and allow it to totally transform us!

Let us walk more assuredly in the Creative Stream of Life by loving fully, deeply, totally the life we have and thus experience the quickening and healing transformation that is possible as we allow the Innate Power, the Eternal Creative Source, to emerge in and through and as us to bring the change, the new awareness that beckons and will ultimately bring fulfillment!

38

A Light Unto Our Path

"The Spirit itself beareth witness with our spirit, that we are the children of God; and if children, then heirs: heirs of God, and joint-heirs with Christ."

Romans 8:16,17

∾

The essential, consistent message of all spiritual teachings and traditions, in all of their myriad forms and ideologies, is that *man is* a child of God. In John 10:34 we read, *"Is it not written in your law, I said ye are Gods?"* This promise, perhaps more than any other single statement, inspires more faith, more hope and more trust in the awakening process than any other similar utterance in the Bible or any other sacred writing.

It is difficult to imagine what life must be like for people who do not know or are not aware of this Divine Inheritance which is available to them. Perhaps this lack of knowing about the inner sacred self and all its potentiality accounts for so much mass confusion, distrust and violence in the world.

To *know* that we are children of God is necessarily a major first step. Knowing suggests an awareness, a cognitive perception that involves our intellect (mental) and our feeling (emotional) self. Knowing also implies a high kind of awareness that is available to us, perhaps called our intuition. Carl Jung, the famous Swiss psychologist whose writings form the basis of that branch of psychological thought that bears his name, suggests repeatedly, in his penetrating research into the depth of the inner man, that our intuitive self knows more about our life process and our beingness than had hitherto been believed or imagined.

To *discover* that we are, indeed, children of the Living God occurs when we face or experience a so-called miracle in our lives. A loved one becomes ill, seriously so. Medical tests prove conclusively that the feared diagnosis is fact. Yet, we refuse to accept as final the confirmed medical opinion and we set forth to pray. We call relatives and friends and ask them to pray also. Most important of all, the person who is ill is him/herself encouraged to reverse their attitude, release their fears and accept healing and the return to wholeness through prayer as well.

As this process comes forward, behold, a remission occurs! A negative chemical state in the body is shifted and the beloved regains his/her health. And we say "A miracle has happened."

This whole process is about discovering that we are children of the Divine Source! The discovery is about learning that we are not victims of a capricious god or fickle fate. We are not destined to die, but to live. The discovery is not forced upon us, nor is it held away from us in some mysterious or mystical manner. It is simply ours to awaken to as we accept and learn about the laws that allow us to utilize our internal energies and take responsibility for our actions and reactions, our habits, our health and our behaviors.

To be a child of God is actualizing what we believe and know to be true. It is a synthesis of knowing the principles of how the universal laws operate and aligning ourselves in such a manner to that knowledge which, in turn, permits us to experience that alignment in the material world; i.e., to be both the chalice and the wine of the spirit in the chalice.

A child that is born with the inner yearning to play a musical instrument, or to paint pictures early in life, *knows* that making music or painting pictures is possible. It's all in the realm of potential. It is yet unawakened. It, the talent or ability, is or remains essentially a possibility!

Discovery comes as the child hears music played on an organ, piano, guitar, flute, harp or whatever and then is given the opportunity to hold an instrument, or to touch the keys, and then to learn about notes. Studies with a teacher follows and the child begins to express his talent through performance and exercising latent abilities. In other words, the potential has been awakened.

Being a child of God, actualizing the potential of the musician (or painter or whatever) is held as the creative focus and occurs when all of the training, all of the practicing to learn how to perform synthesizes into the art. The student ceases being only the student. He becomes one with, he aligns his being with, his Inner Source and demonstrates not only what he has learned by memory or by imitation, but that he can now create consciously and with an awareness of his ability to make his talent real. He no longer sings the song of another or copies the technique of another. He becomes the originator of his own gifts. He has synthesized what he knows and has discovered in his own being a unit that is uniquely his creation, his process, his own experience.

The (spiritual) light upon our path emerges out of our living our life fully and confidently and completely. Light (wisdom, knowledge, guidance or revelation) comes as we use and integrate what we have learned into the very fabric of our lives. Light is always there. We, as God's creations, are never separate from our Creator.

To experience our connection and to keep it vital and energized, we must daily remain open to the power of our intuitive voice. As we learn to listen to that level of our being, we become consciously aware that we are indeed God's children. He speaks to us through our deepest connection with Him and through it becomes the Radiant Light upon our path.

39

The Grand Design for Living

"Finally, brethren, whatsoever things are true, whatsoever things are honest, whatsoever things are just, whatsoever things are pure, whatsoever things are lovely, whatsoever things are of good report; if there be any virtue, and if there be any praise, think on these things."

Philippians 4:8

From this hour I ordain myself loos'd
of limits and imaginary lines,
Going where I list, my own master
total and absolute,
Listening to others, considering
well what they say,
Pausing, searching, receiving
contemplating,
Gently, but with undeniable will
divesting myself of the holds
that would hold me.

Walt Whitman

∾

Dr. Bryant M. Kirkland, pastor of the Fifth Avenue Presbyterian Church in New York City, recently wrote, "Attitude is everything...St. Paul said 'Think on these things', because you color your thoughts with the thoughts you think."

At the end of his life, in prison, St. Paul wrote the words quoted above from Philippians—realizing that man's thoughts run throughout his day, his night, through his activities and quiet times. Since we are constantly energizing our personal environments, ultimately we do become what we think!

New Thought teachings and metaphysical spokespersons of almost all persuasions have long expounded that "thoughts are things". Classes are taught about how to change our lives through changing our thinking. People gather together in groups to learn how to meditate and discover how to quiet their thinking processes, or how to effectively gain control of scattered, unproductive and undisciplined thought. Yet many students of the Inner Way and the deeper spiritual truths have not really mastered the art of changing their *attitudes*. When problems arise, or issues emerge, or people appear in their lives that challenge them, their beliefs or thoughts, these students will often say, "My karma is catching up with me. I cannot master this problem." Or, "My parents (wife, husband or friend) hate me or really dislike me. Therefore, my life is meaningless. It won't work."

The theme, "The Grand Design For Living", suggests that there are many ways to become aligned to the Infinite, to the Unlimited Source of All Good, to overcome feelings of lack, woundedness, hurt, separation or loss. There are numerous ways to master problems, effectively face challenges and permanently release fears! Of the many possibilities, I suggest we focus our thoughts as follows:

1. Change your belief; change the way you think about the issues or situations before you! As a New Thought person, Christian, or follower of any other religious persuasion, only you can be in charge of what you think! The Bible says, "Let the mind of Christ be in you." This suggests that the same Universal Mind that Christ demonstrated is available to us! *Be willing* to look at old issues or problems from a new or different viewpoint. In psychological language this process is called "reframing". It means to take or create a new picture. Our personal *attitude* about this process makes an enormous difference as to how we experience change.

A young wife wrote to her father, saying, "This marriage is no good. I want out! We do not live in a nice place." The wise father wrote back to his beloved daughter simply, "Two men looked out from prison bars - one saw mud, the other saw stars." We can take the high road, the middle road, or the low road in any narrow situation. We *each choose* how we will see or view any problem.

2. Divine Mind is always available to help us gain a new or different experience of our life. It's amazing how many truth students understand/believe this principle, but fail to completely actualize it in their lives.

One approach to using this principle is to relax, become quiet, become open and receptive to this Divine Inflow. Now realize your oneness with God. The open mind and heart whereby one is brought into the receptive attitude is the first necessity. Then, daily, enter the silence. This should be in a place where you will not be agitated by noises or other types of disturbances that could enter through the avenues of your physical senses.

As you begin to realize receiving or being open to the Indwelling Presence, a quiet, peaceful, illuminating power will harmonize your body, soul and mind. This power can then harmonize your life with all life. With practice, you will become open at even deeper levels of Self to the activity of God's Presence (Divine Mind) at the very center of your being. It is at this "place" of quiet receptivity that you are "on the mountaintop" and the voice of God speaks to you! Then as you descend (back into physical consciousness), carry this realization with you. Actualize it. Live in it, walking, working, thinking, waking, sleeping—in all your actions and activities!

The Grand Design for Living becomes a possibility for us as we realize (understand and actualize) that *we are in control* of our lives and our destiny. We shape our future as we are aware of that truth. Our thoughts, our attitudes give shape to our life! God, working in and through us cannot express less than our Ultimate Good! Our grand design involves becoming awakened, conscious and focused upon the business of manifesting more and more of our Godlike nature, day by day, hour by hour, each precious moment by moment of our lifetime!

40

In Tune with the Infinite

> ***"As you live out of loving feelings and Cosmic Ideas, ways and means for your success, joy and fulfillment are revealed ... in the form of ideas and opportunities that are not available when you blame or complain."***
> *The Incredible Cosmic Consciousness Diet*
> **Harvey Cohen, Ph.D.**

∾

It would appear that much of the confusion that reigns supreme in so many sectors of the world, as well as within our individual lives, stems from living out of fear, hurt, blame, and a sense of separation and loss. Most major spiritual teachings, ancient and modern alike, suggest that through appropriate measures man can align himself to the Source of All Life and become open to a conscious partnership with the Universe. Such a relationship with the Universe is filled with peace, promise, fullness, abundance, health, depth and meaning.

We well may ask ourselves, "What is required of me to become attuned to Infinite Power or *The* Infinite Power? What are some of the 'appropriate measures' that are helpful and will enable me to bring an awareness of a deeper connection to the Universe, a greater balance and a richer sense of my life experience?"

As we come to consider these questions, it is necessary for us to begin by first affirming for ourselves a statement of profound spiritual truth. "I (each one of us) am a drop in The Great Ocean of God (Consciousness). I am connected to the Infinite as a wave is connected to the ocean." Initially, even though we may not understand the truth of it or even the possibility of it, we begin by accepting that God is our Larger

True Self, The Infinite Ocean of Consciousness. Allow yourself to gently accept the truth that it is God's good will to love and bless you totally. To then begin to personalize this universal concept, we must recognize another level of acceptance within ourselves as we examine the following series of steps that will lead us to wholeness.

1. Accept that you are in need of help. Stop warring with yourself (and others) over issues, big or small. In the Master Mind process, this step is known as *surrender*. It means yielding, letting go of control (of the ego desire nature) and allowing God to truly take charge of your life. Be patient. Work at letting go daily.

2. Pray. The act of praying suggests a simple, direct, one-on-one conversation with God, very much like speaking aloud to your most trusted companion, parent or friend. Place yourself, your problem, your concern in God's Care. *Accept* and believe that a power greater than yourself—The Infinite Creator of All Life—is responding to you in a most personal, loving way. You are worthy of the help, guidance, assistance, healing or direction you seek!

3. Change your thinking. All spiritual teachings and most psychologists agree that erroneous, self defeating thoughts cause lack, limitation, failure and unhappiness. *Be willing* to have your negative (fear filled) belief system totally changed! Again, this may take time—days, weeks, or even longer to be accomplished. Hold onto your inner willingness to change. Use affirmations. Read inspiring, positive literature. Talk to and associate with inspiring, uplifting, positive minded people.

4. Decide to turn your life over to God! That suggests turning over *everything*, including each conflict, problem, gripe or fault. This decision is made easier when we *let go* (surrender) trying to figure out, analyze and determine with our little personality consciousness why each or any issue is in our life. At this step we stop trying to blame others, or ourselves. It is useless, ultimately, to blame our parents, our family, or other persons.

5. Forgive yourself for all mistakes you have made, whether they were made knowingly or unknowingly. Find and accept a place within yourself where you can *genuinely and willingly* give up the need to rehearse again old wounds, hurts or disappointments. Also, release and/or forgive *everyone* whom you perceive as having injured or harmed you in any manner. Be gentle with yourself at this step. It may take many efforts to really give up holding onto a problem or conflict, an attitude or feeling that is painful or has caused wounding in the past.

6. Ask God for what you need. Again, in a simple direct manner say aloud what specific requests you have for assistance, healing, direction, clarity, wisdom, vision or resolution of a concern, problem or conflict. Even though God knows of your needs before you ask, it is vitally important for your spiritual growth that you place yourself consciously in an attitude of openness and receptivity through the aligning process of asking. As you ask, you begin to turn your attention away from the lack or issue at conflict, toward the Source of the help or answer. Thus, you permit a bridging, or allow an opening for God's Assistance to manifest in your life.

7. Give thanks and accept that God's Answer is emerging in your life. Assume feelings of gratitude, even if you do not see or feel an immediate response or solution. *Trust* that help is on the way. Shifting your attention to thanksgiving creates a space in your heart and, in a larger sense, in your life for the "miracle" you need. Stay focused. Daily, in your quiet time, keep expressing an attitude of thankfulness. Be expectant! Be positive! Allow yourself to feel joyful and continue to trust God for the healing, or the abundance, the guidance, or the assistance that you need. Move in the direction of whatever good you are accepting as manifesting in your life. If you seek better health, for example, do those things which honor the body in terms of proper rest, relaxation, appropriate nutrition and diet, and free the body of stress!

In summation, follow through with these seven steps and do the *best* you can to do your part in this cooperative venture with God in the creative process. Allow yourself to be open to unplanned good, knowing and accepting that God has ways you may not understand. Look to the Source of everything. The Infinite knows how to meet you, at your level of need, on time and in abundance.

It was Goethe who said:

Are you in earnest? Seize this very minute:
What you can do, or dream you can, begin it;
Boldness has genius, power, and magic in it.
Only engage and then mind grows heated;
Begin and then the work will be completed.

41

The Healing Power of Forgiveness

"Blessed is the man that walketh not in the counsel of the ungodly... But his delight is in the law of the Lord; and in his law doth he meditate day and night. And he shall be like a tree planted by the rivers of water, that bringeth forth his fruit in his season; his leaf also shall not wither; and whatsoever he doeth shall prosper."

Psalms 1:1-3

∾

One of life's most difficult areas of personal challenge is to be able to truly forgive (or release) our individual wounds, hurts and pains suffered in our relationships with others. It is difficult to control the tendency to want to "strike back" or to want to "get even" when we perceive that we have been attacked or have suffered some kind of hurtful experience. It seems that pain, having been inflicted, calls for (or justifies) inflicting more pain. Anger expressed, evokes expressions of more anger. Hurled hurts become as sharp rapiers and individuals gird themselves "to fight back against these attacks" which they view as injustices, lies and bigotries. Or, as Shakespeare says in Hamlet, "Whether 'tis nobler in the mind to suffer the slings and arrows of outrageous fortune, or to take arms against a sea of troubles, and by opposing end them?" The worldly view or notion that calls forth the old Mosaic Law, "An eye for an eye; a tooth for a tooth" still seems to be evident in so many ways.

And yet, the major spiritual teachings and traditions say, "Return good for evil, *overcome* anger by love; hatred never ceases by hatred, but by love." (Hindu) The Buddhist says, "If a man foolishly does me wrong, I will return him protection of my undying love." The Bible teaches, *"But love ye your enemies ... and ye shall be the children of the Highest; for He is kind unto the unthankful and to the evil."* (Luke 6:35) And again in Luke 6:37, *"Judge not and ye shall not be judged; condemn not, and ye shall not be condemned; forgive and ye shall be forgiven."*

What does this seem to suggest? Some of what is implied is set forth in the following points as suggestions for personal growth and transformation to learn to experience the real healing power available to us as we practice forgiveness:

1. Forgiveness implies releasing, letting go, giving up an attachment to some *idea, feeling* or perception. Metaphysically, we give to the Source whatever is out of balance, out of step, out of rhythm or synchronization in life. In giving to Source (God), we let go of our little individual will attempts to rectify, to "set the balance". We allow (surrender to) God and His Will to handle the inequity.

2. Loving our enemies,—returning good for evil, ... implies the spiritual teaching that since we *each* are a child of light (of God), to love our enemies means to focus on their sacred nature, their Divine Nature, and not to perceive them as separate from the Source. It means that we see more than what we had perceived as "the mistake" or "evil". It is our individual responsibility to remind ourselves first, and others second, of our Higher Selves. We remind by acting, living and being in all ways that we express our highest good—always!

This relates to the concept that what we send forth from ourselves on an energy level (an inner level) returns to us. What we sow, we reap. If we want to live in balance, then we must not send forth anything on any level that would disturb that state. In truth teachings we are taught to say, "I am loving". This implies that we are expressing our capacity to *be* an instrument of, a vehicle for, the activity of love in our lives.

Ralph Waldo Trine writes in *In Tune With the Infinite*, "When we come to fully realize the great fact that...evil,...error and sin with their consequent sufferings come through ignorance, then wherever we see a manifestation of these in whatever form, if our hearts are right, we will have compassion...compassion will then change itself into love and love will manifest itself in kindly service." *"From a point of Light within the Mind of God,"* as *"Light streams forth into the minds of men,"* the reality of each person's ultimate, highest nature will be shown to exist in the most profound ways. Instead of attacking our "enemies" (read teachers), we will support them. We will offer help and love, not retaliation and hate. Truly, we will then come from a place of fullness and not from a place of lack or limitation!

Forgiveness brings release—to ourselves and to others. We will no longer hold the hurt or woundedness. We will yield it to the Source. We will quit energizing it. And, as we do so, we will become free. Free to continue our journey. Free to serve, free to grow, deepen and expand, develop and awaken to ever new, ever higher levels of ourselves.

The true healing (or return to wholeness) in forgiveness is that we give ourselves permission to once again, and more profoundly, identify the Spirit of Infinite Love. The *very moment* we become conscious of it, or recognize ourselves as being one with it, we will become so focused in and filled with love and we will truly see only good, wholeness and love in all. As we become more and more conscious of this oneness, in ourselves and with all others, ... in other words, as we more and more establish this loving connectedness, we will be unable to render harm, or be revengeful or destructive to any one or any thing!

As we come to more fully *realize* the great truth of the oneness of all life, that all are partakers of the Divine Source, and that the same life is in each person, plant and creature, then prejudices will vanish, hatred will cease, and Love will reign supreme. It is then that we can say, "I salute the God within" and at the innermost depths of our being we will recognize the truth, the freeing, transforming truth that God within has come forth - into action, in, through and as our lives!

42

New Frontiers

"The Kingdom of God is inside of you and it is outside of you. When you come to know yourselves, then you will be known, and you will realize that you are the sons of the living Father. But if you will not know yourselves, then you dwell in poverty, and it is you who are that poverty..."

Gospel of Thomas from *The Gnostic Gospels*
Elaine Pages

∾

Frontier is defined, "the incompletely developed region of a field of knowledge, feeling, etc." By implication, that which permits an extension of, expansion of, or development of an idea, construct or pattern.

We enter a new frontier whenever we embark upon a new project, start a different job, or set out to achieve a fresh goal. Therefore, such things as choosing another geographical area in which to live, or experimenting with a newly acquired ability such as operating a computer or creating and packaging a video film would require stretching one's personal, physical, emotional, mental and psychological limits. That, too, is moving into a new frontier.

In the larger arena of life, biologists are researching the DNA structure and pondering how understanding it and experimenting to alter it will possibly affect human life. Medical science has given us the gifts of improving upon the quality of life and actually extending life through its marvels - new (exchanged) hearts, liver and lung transplants, donor kidneys, restored eyesight (different corneas), etc. Diseases emerge that trigger medical research to find antidotes to life threatening conditions, such as the AIDS viruses. Business failures, bankruptcies and foreclosures have led to creative forms of financing and often to very new kinds of business relationships and enterprises. In each of the areas mentioned, a "new frontier" came forward to challenge exploration in order that life might continue, or could develop or change to accommodate the issue, or problem.

In the field of consciousness studies, a host of men and women have explored altered states of awareness. The body of research is now ponderous and extremely comprehensive. Dr. Charles Tart, an experimental and transpersonal psychologist, author of several books on consciousness and a faculty member in the psychology department of the University of California at Davis, is one of the few people whose work commands respect in both the broad scientific and spiritually oriented communities. He suggests that we need to learn how to "wake up" from our ordinary states of awareness and intelligently enter and function at higher levels of consciousness. This function, claims Dr. Tart, is really the opportunity we each have for extraordinary development.

Spiritual teachers from the major world traditions have all told us that "The kingdom of God is within." Consistently, modern researchers into paranormal states, or altered states of consciousness have suggested the same teaching and have opened (for us) new frontiers in awareness of our true or real nature. What, then, can we assume, what can we do about allowing ourselves to really accomplish this "kingdom of God within" in ways that are constructive, useful and spiritually affirming?

1. Our personal life is our personal resource. If we are to awaken, we must examine our life and its purposing. We must learn to probe deeply into our beingness and then we must carefully examine whatever emerges in that personal arena that reflects the nature of our more subtle makeup, or "spiritual self".

2. We must develop practices that support this awakening process. Some such useful practices are: prayer, meditation., yoga and chanting. We cannot enter a greater (expanded) state of consciousness if we are ruled exclusively by our ordinary consciousness and awareness, our normal day-to-day focus on chores, duties, responsibilities and personal issues.

3. We must give ourselves permission to pursue new frontiers in our lives. If a new relationship is really tugging at us, then we must provide space—internal space (permission) and external space (opportunity)—for that to occur. If we are yearning to return to school, regardless of our ages or personal circumstances or concerns, we must put forth the effort to move in that direction of enhancing the totality of our being. We must foster and augment our potentials. We will do this as we give ourselves permission to move into uncharted areas of our lives in the particular arenas of study we are drawn to.

4. Let us act in the moment. That means we will stop building monuments to the past by inordinate celebration of the accomplishments or the failures it held. We will honor the accomplishments. We will accept our failures. We will move on. And, by extension, we will not "live in the future," either. Power is contained in the now. Let us act on what life presents to us moment by moment ... making our plans and charting our courses as goals and objectives to be realized.

5. To awaken to "the kingdom of God within" means that we will **learn to live life from the inside out!** We must submit our little wills to God's higher will. We must surrender ourselves, all that we are and all that we hope to become, to God, or Pure Being, and then allow ourselves to be guided to do, to live, to be our very best! That does not mean we will ignore the advice of spiritual teachers or wise persons. It does mean that we will follow the particular spiritual disciplines that inspire us individually and that will lead us to our personal transformation.

We must remember, however, that none of us can experience our awakening, or expansion of consciousness—we cannot stretch into new areas of becoming or being by allowing ourselves to act only on the vision or direction of others. If we are to grow and deepen, unfold and expand, we must learn to trust our own nature, our own creativity, our own gifts and our own talents—and we must explore them!

New frontiers, then, are simple and complex. For the awakening individual, dealing with life's issues and challenges is not as difficult. They are faced with strength and courage.

The awakening person learns to cooperate with life. He/she has discovered that the "secret" of awakening is in overcoming, and ultimately yielding to what life's thrust brings. For the "unawakened or struggling" individual, dealing with life's slings and arrows converts to denial, resistance, anger and often, violence! The pain becomes too great. Coping with life isn't seen as a possible or a viable choice.

Yet, we are reminded over and over again that we can make a choice. The Kingdom of God is within us. What a magnificent promise! Altered states and expanded states notwithstanding, it is only when *we choose to begin* whatever action is called for or needed that we find a new doorway (of consciousness), or a new frontier (of possibility) opening to us. But what guides us in choosing our directions? If we rely solely on our human intellect, our reasoning, we can easily make mistakes. However, when we turn to the Infinite Possibilities of intuitional guidance, we are divinely led. *"I will instruct thee and teach thee in the way which thou shalt go; I will guide thee with mine eye."* (Psalm 32:8)

43

Making Your Life Work

"If you keep my commandments, ye shall abide in my love; even as I have kept my Father's commandments, and abide in his love." **St. John 13:10**

∾

Recently, an exasperated student of spiritual truth exclaimed, "I know how to make my life work, but I can't seem to do it! Where am I going wrong?"

Probably most of us, at some juncture of our life ... perhaps even very recently—have uttered a similar statement. With the result, oftentimes, that doubt, worry, fear and/or disappointment creep into our lives, our thinking and our spiritual quest. Such responses lead us away from Jesus' teaching, "If you keep my commandments, ye shall abide in my love." At such times, we lose the sense of connection with the spiritual dimension of our being, we lose (momentarily, or however long our confusion may last) the sense of belonging or being in the flow and that God is available, that love or hope or help is, indeed, on the way and rightfully ours! Not to overstate it, but at such times we tend to get bogged down in the "mechanics" of spiritual truth and what we're doing wrong.

Knowing the universal (spiritual) laws, or studying and learning about them is profoundly important. Attending classes, belonging to a church (synagogue, organization or whatever) that teaches such principles is helpful. Regular attendance at public worship is important. That is to say, repeated exposure to truth teachings in a learning environment where we associate with others of like mind is very useful.

Whether we individually have a momentary lapse of being in the flow, or whether we are students who may not have actually experienced that desired state, it is vitally important that we do not mistake an intellectual understanding of principles for that deeper, inner experience, that sense of connection with the Source. Going to classes, gathering information, studying universal principles is interesting, but then comes the work of putting our understanding into practice.

For example, if the current lesson in our personal life is to learn how to let go (forgive, release), how much data do we need? How many books, classes, seminars, churches, teachers, etc., are needed to reveal the teaching? Someone once said, "We need to be exposed to a principle or lesson over and over again until we can demonstrate it!" Well, be that as it may, more information about the need to forgive does not change one's behavior. Reading about forgiveness, hearing about forgiveness, being told about the process of forgiveness does not bring about forgiveness.

Rather, making life work is actually actively cooperating with the principle of life that aids the desired change to manifest. Whenever our lives "get out of focus", when we encounter restrictions and limitations, when things just don't seem to go right, we must always come back to basics. Do we understand the principles?

Continuing with our discussion of the lesson of forgiveness, we must be willing to be changed at depth, to really give up or cease hurtful, angry, resentful, revenge-filled, pain-filled thoughts and feelings. There are many techniques, from prayer and visualization exercises to meditation and therapeutic tools, to help this process come about.

Keeping the commandments suggests ongoing application of universal spiritual laws. Love (acceptance), God's Grace, unlimited Good, abundance are ever open to us and will continue to flow into increasingly more areas of our lives —*if*, as Jesus told us, *if* we keep his commandments. Quite simply, this means we must stay at it. We must continue to work at the commandment of forgiveness, for example, daily, consistently. It is not sufficient after one affirmation of forgiveness to assert, "There, I've done it! I've made my effort!"

Working with the commandments is an ongoing *process*! As we, through study and consistent application, work with, cooperate and align with spiritual principles, we can then eventually claim our good by the examples of our lives.

Sai Baba says, "Begin the day with love, live the day with love and end the day with love." Is this a "commandment"? Perhaps. Perhaps it is his teaching that it is possible for us to love all the time and live from a place in our consciousness that allows us to experience love all of the time.

Returning again to the lesson of forgiveness, if we say "I forgive you", "I forgive myself," but secretly we hold onto some hurtful memory, or we harbor some thought of revenge, we are not free. We are still in bondage to the limitations of our little self, our egoic self. We may want love. We may strive for love. We may affirm it. We may tell ourselves or others how important love is, but we will not fully demonstrate love in our life if we are still knowingly or unknowingly holding onto woundedness and unresolved issues from our past.

And, as we master one lesson, isn't there always another lesson awaiting our attention? Aren't we always being presented with our lessons in different guises to test whether or not we really made the commandments work in our lives?

Making our life work is not a striving or an anxious, fearful approach to life to please God, or to discover the principles by which the worlds coexist. It is more that we recognize God as the immanent as well as the transcendent. To the degree that we can make this recognition, we are able to partake of His Life and Power. We are able to experience a direct connection to His Presence—in us!

Love might be said to be the key to this sense of connectedness. Abiding in love is in reality available to us, to everyone. It is not the special selection by God of a mate, a friend, lover or companion, but the openness that allows us to see the larger dimension of the Infinite Life in which all people are included. Love frees us to serve, to be receptive, to be attuned, to be aware that we are in harmony and rhythm, we are in flow with the universe about us.

Making your life work is about making your life a vessel of Love. As you let go of personality self and let God crown you with His indwelling Presence, your light outshines the sun and your life is a song of the cosmos.

44

Goal Setting - Planting the Seeds

"But let him ask in faith, nothing wavering. For he that wavereth is like a wave of the sea driven with the wind and tossed." **James 1:6**

∾

Beginning a new task, starting a new endeavor, or attempting a new direction in life is often viewed at the outset as a monumental effort. There is a tendency for people to anticipate the problems that may (or may not) be involved. They focus instead on their fears and insecurities. And worse, they allow their resistance to the new project or endeavor (opportunity) to totally eclipse its possibilities. Thus, descent into anger or depression, frustration or denial is the result, which repeats the pattern of other efforts that ended in futility. The big stumbling block is the remembrance of former efforts that met with resistance, or were blocked or bungled. Each new task or endeavor thus laid aside, dropped or dumped leaves its residue of hurt, disappointment, confusion, frustration and self-doubt.

Spiritual teachers the world over have offered some amazing insights and truly profound teachings regarding this state of being (or state of mind, state of feeling). For instance, Jesus said, *"Ask and it shall be given unto you; seek and ye shall find; knock and it shall be opened unto you. For everyone that asketh receiveth and he that seeketh findeth and to him that knocketh, it shall be opened."* (Matthew 7:7,8)

In beginning any task or endeavor, *we need to ask.* Let's explore the states or conditions of asking, seeking and finding.

The American College Dictionary defines asking as : "to seek to be informed about; to make inquiry." To ask, then, suggests an attitude of openness and receptivity. It's active. *We* reach out. *We* make an effort. *We* create a space within our life, our activities, our work, our relationships that suggests allowing room for a new idea or new insight, a new direction or growth.

Inquiry suggests a probing, investigation into something, an effort to find out, to pierce or discover, to become informed. Inquiry requires intention, an act of will fueled by feeling (desire) and some significant personal involvement, some personal time (and perhaps resources), and a willingness to learn.

Seeking involves doing, acting or looking from a place of clear motive or purpose. To seek means to go in search of or to try to find out by examination or by exploration endeavors.

Now, we've moved from creating space for something new in our lives to actively seeking it. We are actively pursuing a new task, starting a new endeavor, or attempting a new direction in life by our planning (Goals), and participation in study, in work efforts and in deeds.

Finding implies or suggests bringing into our lives the thing(s) we seek—or being able to recognize that which we seek as emerging in our lives. Further, it allows us to actually own (accept) our discoveries, to make them our own. That means that we no longer see them as outside of ourselves; we see them, feel and know them as part(s) of our ongoing life experience in a harmonious and balanced way.

We have more or less been defining terms. Let us recapitulate the stages involved with Goal Setting—Planting the Seeds.

Goals are the desires, purposes, things, objectives that focus our attention. Whenever we ask (of the universe), we are in the first stage of goal setting. Here we actually formulate what it is that we want, desire or need. We create a sacred space in our lives to embrace it and become receptive to the possibility of its realization. Here we open up to the Source of All Life and say, "I'm willing to reach out, to begin, to dare. I am an open channel of your blessings. Use me."

The second stage of goal setting is seeking. Now we actually *do* something toward fulfilling our objective. We formulate a plan. We take action-oriented steps to discover what is needed, desired or sought for. If we seek a deeper spiritual life, we take action. We study inspirational writings, we pray, meditate or practice a physical discipline such as yoga or Tai-Chi Chuan. Perhaps we want to improve a relationship, heal an old one, develop a new career, or go to some exotic part of the world. Once our goal is clear to us, we must next consider what steps we are willing to put into action, what efforts we must put into play in a physical direction. This will vary for each individual and whatever their objective. After planting the seeds, next comes a time of germination in which we must maintain a positive outlook that a positive harvest (result) will be the outcome. This is not a passive "wait and see" attitude. It involves all parts of us ... physically, emotionally, mentally and spiritually.

The third stage of goal setting, or planting the seeds, is finding or discovery. We find, perhaps, that our goal as first defined needs revision or refinement. We may actually have to change it, modify or rethink it, or drop it. Maybe we discover that part of our goal or focus is realized, but a part is not. Sometimes we find that what we thought was our direction or goal (or focus) isn't at all what we wanted or needed or desired. Finding also implies an ownership of our results. If we find, for instance, that we can make more money and yet cannot hold onto what we make or cannot manage it wisely, we must own (integrate) that part of ourselves that feels worthy and deserving—in this case, of more money—with that part of ourselves that feels unworthy, perhaps even lazy and indifferent to work and responsibility. Ownership of life experiences is significant to and valuable to our solid psychological and spiritual well-being.

To learn from our experiences is one of the most important keys in our overall spiritual journey. Because goals give us direction, clarity, focus and a sense of purpose, we can measure our movement (or lack of it) across the sea of our whole life. Goals are signposts heralding possibilities. Successful projects and accomplishments emerge in our lives because we are inner-directed and outer-directed in a balanced action or activity. Goals are seeds we are planting to harvest in the fullness of time - in every season of the year - in all the years of our lives.

We are each a seed in God's garden of perfection. He has tilled the soil of our hearts, minds and souls. The Living Waters of His Spirit nurture us. And he harvests us in our realization of our at-one-ment, in our growth into the Light of our Christhood. We bless God's goal of your perfection.

45

Exploring Practical Metaphysics

"We only assume ourselves to be individualized beings. We falsely conceive that we are bound to a mind and a body. Our real, larger nature is God. It is not correct to assert, 'I am God'. It is correct to know, 'God is expressing as me, as the ocean expresses the wave'. Until we awaken to the truth about our true being and our relationship with the ocean of consciousness, we wander through the corridors of space and time in an unconscious manner." **Roy Eugene Davis**
Open Your Life to Infinite Good

∾

Metaphysics can be described as the science of the study of Being. It orders, classifies and arranges various systems of thought regarding man's inner being into specific teachings such as espoused by Unity, Divine Science, Science of Mind, etc., and many independent truth teachers. What sets metaphysics apart from other forms of philosophy is its emphasis upon the possibility of a personal identification with an inner power, a divine presence, a universal principle, the Father-Mother God, Ultimate Reality! This identification and connection is ever available to all sincere seekers of Light (wisdom) anywhere who make the conscious effort to become more aware of their inner nature and relationship to the Source!

Since metaphysics is really about the study of the science of being, no serious approach to the study of our inner nature can be denied. There is a great diversity of systems of study which, when approached separately as part of the total science of metaphysics, can sometimes be confusing and seemingly contradictory. For example, currently there are "channelers" of supposedly enlightened entities whose "teachings" they claim are ultimate truth. There are self help exponents from rebirthers to proponents of the powers of crystals. Psychics, energy healers, practitioners of Zen Buddhism, of yoga, meditation, of mind control—each claims that their system offers a viable approach for the study and development of our inner being.

In a larger sense, all approaches to the study of our inner being have validity. We cannot arbitrarily determine for any individual other than ourselves which system is for the greater good or highest level of awakening. What we must each strive to determine for ourselves is what is the end result that any teaching or system proposes. In other words, where does it lead us?

To that end, some significant questions might be appropriate to help provide a logical framework as we individually try to understand our personal journey and sense of discovery as we explore the sometimes confusing and sometimes seemingly contradictory world of metaphysical study:

1. Is the teaching based upon a serious (old or new) scientific inquiry? Is the material offered open to question or reexamination outside the confines of its founder, teachers or exponents? Has the founder (if there is one) set forth his ideas carefully and clearly? Can they be replicated? Are the teachings demonstrable?

2. Does the teaching or system rely heavily on aids, or tools, or "crutches" such as devices or objects (either natural or man-made) or techniques or structures? Any of these can be useful but should not be ends in and of themselves, nor should they be critically ongoing and limiting one to the structure of the teaching or system of science. (See point 7 below.)

3. The claim of many metaphysical teachings, as well as all spiritual teachings, is that use of the system will lead to a more positive lifestyle, freedom from hurt, from guilt and pain into greater states of inner peace, love and wholeness with the Divine. In short, we will actually come to know our true identity and our relationship to God. Does this, in fact, appear to be the case with the teacher, the members of the classes, groups or organizations that espouse the practices and apply the principles of the systems(s)?

4. Does the teaching ultimately lead to spiritual awakening? To greater Transformation? To a deeper, higher, greater —yea, all-consuming relationship to the Source, Supreme Being, Infinite Intelligence, Ultimate Reality? Many teachers/teachings promise this goal. Do they deliver? Again, does this appear to be the truth with the teacher, the members of the classes, groups or organizations?

5. Do the teachers/teachings reflect a statement that is centered in Love, active in service, committed to express God (Life, Universal Principle) in the noblest or finest sense? Does the teacher/teaching support and express the most altruistic ideals while yet demonstrating their reality in practical ways to everyday life?

6. Is the teaching truly effective and workable? Is it practical? Useful? Demonstrable? If so, how does it work in daily life with actual life issues, concerns, problems? If the teacher or teaching offers escapism, "pie-in-the-sky", or avoidance of personal responsibility, I suggest that you reconsider your involvement.

7. Does the system or teaching *overly* rely on techniques? Processes? Tools? Does it create a dependency structure of more and more classes, more and more training to gain a "higher state of being", or "ultimate awareness"? If so, reconsider. Processes, techniques and tools are necessary to aid the student in the awakening journey. However, since each of us is inherently an individual creation of the Divine Idea, be aware that techniques alone are not a substitute for the process of discovering and/or claiming our true spiritual nature. In other words, a process or technique may lead us to our inner being, but the process or technique is *not* the truth or real identity of our being. Study, disciplined lives and daily application of spiritual principles are the foundation of inner growth and awakening.

Many major metaphysical systems have developed or grown into large organizations such as Religious Science or Science of Mind, Divine Science and Unity. Currently, many independent teachers such as Johnny Coleman, Barbara King and Roy Eugene Davis have built powerful ministries based upon truth teachings (or metaphysical approaches), but have removed the allure of gimmicks, gee haws and tinsel-coated pedagogics that promise life changing results over a weekend, in a single seminar, or in one special event. All of these groups and individuals focus upon the following to help make metaphysics a practical and useful science of the study of being:

a. Man is a spiritual being capable of demonstrating his higher, loftier nature within the context of his life at all times ... wherever, whenever.

b. *We* are responsible for our lives. There is no one who is coming to our rescue!

c. We are centered in God. Wherever we are, God is. Therefore, no bogeyman is waiting to mislead us. The devil or evil we fear may be our own misperception of our directions, intents or our lack of connectedness to the Presence of God in every area of our lives.

d. Every day we have the opportunity to learn from the past and, thus, to empower the future we are creating!

e. Universal Principles (or Laws) can be demonstrated. As we learn and understand a principle, we activate it within our life's expression. (For example: as we learn about electricity, we learn how to use it, how to make it work for us.)

f. We each progress on the spiritual path at our own inner rate of speed. There is no more, there is no less of God in anyone. We each progress according to our individual ability to express the nature of Divine Reality *in, through* and *as* our lives!

For each of us, exploring the intriguing, fascinating and ultimately spiritually rewarding study of metaphysical science is an *individual* journey. Within that context, each of the major systems has developed guidelines, a series of steps that will help the beginner as well as the more informed seeker to learn, unfold and awaken. Cautions, such as given in the seven points preceding, are appropriate and amazingly helpful when heeded. Finally, in its broadest terms, metaphysical awareness will potentially enable and empower each person to access and use his/her inner power in useful and practical everyday measures, leading to ultimate self-realization.

46

Expressions of the Grateful Heart

Gratitude is defined as "an appreciative awareness *and* thankfulness, as for kindness shown or something received." All spiritual traditions and teachings suggest that in order to experience a deeper connectedness, a deeper consciousness, or a more complete and direct relationship to the Divine (the Source, the Father-Mother God), it is essential to encourage and nurture within one's self this "appreciative awareness". That is to say, we must *daily* acknowledge and express our thanks for the gift of life and *everything* ("good", "bad" and "indifferent") that is in our life at that moment.

At first glance, that might appear to be a pretty far-fetched proposition for some individuals, depending upon their circumstances. It might sound like a very idealistic but unrealistic idea, depending upon one's understanding of reality.

Behind all of life's circumstances are lessons. Behind all lessons and appearances of reality is Ultimate Reality. It is to That that we must learn to express our gratitude for all things.

Within the world of day-to-day living, yes, gratitude is often hard won. Learning of a job loss is seldom met with thankfulness. Discovering that a loved one is in the terminal stages of cancer or some other equally horrendous illness would not appropriately be cause for celebration. Passing through loss - be it divorce, separation from someone we love, or death - hardly merits our "appreciative awareness" or an attitude of gratitude. Handling stressful, complicated relationships, or missing out on the experience of a meaningful relationship is often very painful and traumatic in an on-going sense.

How, then, does one express any kind of appreciative awareness in the midst of such pain and sense of lack or inharmony? How can one become open to the gifts of the heart beyond the feelings of loss and woundedness?

Remember, behind all appearances (circumstances) is Ultimate Reality. The following steps are suggestions of ways that allow for Expressions of the Grateful Heart to emerge gradually and be expressed within our life.

1. Take inventory of your life. Make a list of every condition or circumstance in your personal life. The purpose of this listing is to help establish some order and thus gain a perspective of what is contained within your life's framework. Do not assign "good" or "bad" values to listings.

2. Write in detail an experience within the recent past that has pleased you, for whatever reason. It can be job related or family related. It can be very intimate or known to many people. Set forth the details of the event or occasion you select with clarity, honesty, integrity and as much as it is within your ability to do so, describe your *personal reactions* to the experience.

3. Evaluate your reactions to step 2. To evaluate means to weigh, to consider, to reflect upon *why* you felt pleased or favorably disposed toward the person, event or experience. Again set forth your perceptions as clearly and as precisely as possible.

4. Choose what you consider to be the most important area, now take the inventory you made in step 1 and or arena of your life (to you) and write out, in some detail, *why* you feel the particular way you do about the events or circumstances you selected. *After* writing your response(s), ask yourself, "Is this condition (or situation) serving me in my life? If so, how? If not, am I free to release it?" If you believe you are free to release it, do so.

5. Begin daily to give thanks for the little, ordinary, every day things in your life—a smile from a neighbor, a kindness performed by a stranger, a place to live, food to eat, awareness that you are human and have many options in life—ultimately progressing to other things or conditions as soon as that is possible.

6. Develop some relationship to God, the Infinite in life. Pray. Meditate. Chant. Sing! Praise. Take a walk. Smell a flower and savor its delicate fragrance as long as possible. Note and appreciate something creative—a gaily decorated store window, a magnificently set diamond ring, a painting or fine art drawing, a sunrise or sunset, or even pouring rain! Do this every day. Do it in your own way. Begin to look at your surroundings and your environment differently and you will be amazed how different your life will begin to appear to you.

7. Accept what life has given you and *learn* to use it. The old cliche still applies, "If life hands you a lemon, make lemonade!" An experience is no more or no less than you make it. Accepting and working with what life offers is the real beginning of the dimension of gratitude.

Gratitude, then, is an attitude that is reflective of an inner state or condition of being. It comes about through being open to life's impulse in us, around us and as us. The experience of a grateful heart triggers or ignites an opening to life's sacred essence everywhere we are.

We do not need a special person to make us appreciative. A particular condition or set of circumstances does not need to occur to provide our happiness, fulfillment, security or freedom from pain or stress.

What is needed more is a certain receptivity to the idea that God's Presence is already within us—*now*! As an attitude of thankfulness is developed, we can more fully tap the pulse of the sacred, the holy, the very Life Stream of the Infinite itself in all aspects of living, from the mundane to the sublime. The voice of intuition which will guide us into a healing Oneness of perfect right action, right where we are, is always available to us. We have but to let it be.

47

The Many Faces of God

"And God said, Let us make man in our image, after our likeness. And God created man in his own image, in the image of God created he him." **Genesis 1:26,27**

Our birth is but a sleep and a forgetting;
The Soul that rises with us, our life's Star,
Hath had elsewhere, its setting,
And cometh from afar.
Not in entire forgetfulness
And not in utter nakedness,
But trailing clouds of glory do we come
From God, who is our home.

William Wordsworth
Intimations of Immortality

∾

Perhaps one of the most significant spiritual forces of the 20th century is that mankind is once again "discovering" or being reminded of the universal Truth that "The kingdom of God is within you." But even as various and sundry teachers and churches bring forth the message of "God within", individually we may also be confronted with many different, and what can be uncomfortable, choices. Which teacher is the right one for me? Whose "channeled revelations" are the highest, clearest or most meaningful? Which system offers the "correct" and "official" doctrine of truth? Which church is centered in divine principle? Does the "New Age"—a somewhat ubiquitous term—apply to all, some or none of the study called metaphysics? Indeed, does metaphysics belong in the "New Age"? Which weekend, week-long, two-week or month-long, six-month or year-long training will hasten complete and total transformation and thus lead to enlightenment? Do I give up being Christian, or Jewish, or Buddhist to discover my true relationship with the Source, God within? The list of questions might go on and on endlessly. The deeper the search, the more we question the process of the search.

As some people begin their metaphysical search, they discover that many of their answers can be found in the study of science, such as biology, chemistry, mathematics or physics. For example, Quantum Physics, at its core, suggests the oneness of man with all life, all life forms (mineral, plant, animal and human).

Others find direction in exploring the varied psychological, mythological, sociological or parapsychological studies and approaches to the question of who is man. Each study suggests through its specialized focus that man can discover unlimited worlds of knowledge and inner meaning about the nature of his relationship to these particular areas of his life.

Learning about God, The Infinite Source of All Life, emerges out of all areas of exploring and *experiencing our own individual life*! God is the Infinite Source. Life is about discovering our personal relationship to that Source. Children might be made aware that advanced schooling exists called "university" or "college". However, six, seven, eight or even ten year olds cannot comprehend what college or university levels of education are all about. So it is with our spiritual understanding. When we first become aware of something of the nature of Spiritual Reality, we may have a sense or feeling of what that suggests or encourages in us. However, we will not understand the implications of its broader, larger dimensions until we begin to experience our personal relationship to the Source in our lives.

Discovery comes through the careful study and observation of our own life. Where are our skills? Talents? What systems of intellectual pursuits speak to us? Do we relate to our environment through our sense of touch? Are we auditorily more acute? Are we visually oriented? Does music "speak" to us? Art? Or, are we more scientifically prone—analyzing, critical? Do we respond to nature—water, earth, desert, mountains? Do we relate to animals? Are we sensitive to children?

On the path of self-discovery we must also necessarily examine our weaknesses or limitations as they are perceived. Do we demonstrate anger, fear or resentment? Do our actions bespeak envy or jealousy? Do we have a tendency toward being revengeful? Perhaps even violent? As they may exist, seeing these traits in ourselves for what they are is *part* of discovery.

Awareness, then, is about discerning that our limitations represent blocked energies which are in reality gifts, disguised or masked. We have but to learn how to unmask them and reveal their true essence.

For example: Jealousy is a fearful, possessive attitude one may have toward a man, woman or condition in one's life. As long as we are fearful (jealous), we are trapped by fear. When we are able to overcome our fear and release it, we are then made aware of what is rightfully ours. No one can take from us another person or condition which is truly, rightfully ours.

The many faces of God become revealed to us as we tap the innermost and outermost perimeters of our nature. We alone, apparently, of all of God's creations seem to be able to discern the *purpose, nature* of and *relationship* of our sacred essence to all other life. Every great enterprise man establishes has been brought about through his awareness of and response to this Divine sharing; his agriculture, industries, arts, sciences, systems of education, jurisprudence and government. Each of us can take into our business, personal, social or spiritual endeavors a vast resource. As we choose to use this resource, it can supply us with better ideas, keener insight into opportunities before us, and a greater sense of honor and justice, of compassion, love and understanding.

Life reveals itself to us through *our experience* of it! There is no place we can go, no direction we can take where God is not. Therefore, all teachers, sages, masters and mystics make their contributions. Each reflects a facet or aspect of the face of God. Metaphysics is simply one way to discover the nature of God's presence within us. It is, unto itself, not Truth, but rather a useful system to become aware of truth. No one system has all of the answers. If that was so, there would be one teaching upon all the earth pertinent to the knowledge of God. God reveals Himself in unlimited millions of forms.

We cannot hasten our enlightenment through in-depth seminars or trainings. What we can do is to create a receptive atmosphere in which we may learn to discover who we are, who we truly are, and thus be empowered to soar among the stars!

Beauty, truth, goodness, honesty, light, love—are images upon the face of God. Indeed, we are made in His image. We are part of the wonder, part of the awesome and profound. We are part of the beauty, the love, goodness and unfolding light. It was thus so in the beginning. It is so in the now and shall be so for ever. You, dear friend, are one of the many faces of God!

48

Renewing the Miracle of Christmas

"Ye are the light of the world. A city that is set on a hill cannot be hid. ... Let your light so shine before men, that they may see your good works and glorify your father which is in heaven." **Matthew 5:14,16**

∾

Those ancient words of Jesus the Christ ring out anew across the centuries. "*Ye* are the light of the world.... Let your light so shine..." What a magnificent promise they carry! What a profound, deeply spiritual truth is revealed to us.

And yet, sometimes amidst all of the holiday festivities related to the celebration of Christmas, there is an eclipse of Jesus' words. On the one hand, we are led in psalter and song to worship "Christ the New Born King". On the other hand, somehow we often fail to hear or we forget the message that Christ came to bring. We see the Christ as special and separate, as a Savior and God-incarnate man. Once this view is established in our thinking, we tend to see Christ as outside us, apart from us and therefore, not available to us, except perhaps in some very special circumstances or conditions such as in meditation, prayer, inspirational state or holy place.

When Jesus (the Christ) said, "Ye are the light of the world....," he was talking about the qualities of each person's inner essence—our radiant, sacred, holy self. Light is a metaphor, a symbol of that which cannot be named. Yet, light is also a quality of energy—energy having many qualities (heat, radiance, density, velocity, cohesion, fusion, etc.). If we "are the light of the world," metaphorically or symbolically, we, *each one* of us, carry an imprint of the Divine within us. The light, or the demonstration of life's impulse as light (or energy) is within us. Again, we "...are the light..." We always have the opportunity to express that light or essence wherever or whenever we seek to do so.

Jesus went further to say, "Let your light so shine before men, that they may see your good works and glorify your father which is in heaven." If we are the light, and act upon the light impulse from within (the Divine within), we shall do good works.

Good works flow from those who are open to the Presence of God, (the Divine Essence), in their lives. Good works emerge not because we are "earning salvation" or stacking up "good karma." Good works are not efforts of our ego motivations or causes. Rather, good works are demonstrations of clarity, honesty, integrity, truthfulness, wisdom and vision that emerge from our deepest inner being, born of the desire to know, love and serve God.

If we accept Jesus' words as the basis for a spiritual truth teaching, how can it affect our lives and the quality of life as we live it? Let us consider....

1. As much as possible, each of us must be an example of the activity or expression of the inner Presence or light within the context of our own life. We do this in everything we think, do and say. We do this through and by our example in handling relationships, business matters, personal affairs, health issues, and so forth and so on. In other words, we attempt to live from an inner-directed, loving, sacred place and bring forward into our individual lives examples of the highest and best, deepest spiritual teachings that we know and are able to practice.

2. Learn to see all mankind as children of God and expressions of the Divine. This may require a huge shift in thinking because we may not be accustomed to viewing others in this manner. For example, when we see or read about people committing violent acts upon one another, or abusing one another, our tendency may be first to judge them and condemn their actions. For most people, in all probability, it would require a big stretch in their makeup to forgive a robber, a rapist, a murderer or assassin. Yet, in every person, no matter how perverted or evil, no matter how deeply buried it may be,

still and all a holy seed exists, the light of God is there. The spark of Divinity animates that life as well as our own. We are each called upon to see that light in one another, in *all* others. We are called upon to know this reality and to affirm it. We must know it and affirm it first for ourselves and be an example of that light and thus illustrate it to others.

Illustrating indicates a better way. It does not rescue or try to save. It reveals, supports and reflects what is known inside.

3. Reject the idea that the Light of Christ or Inner Light is the special domain of one group, one teacher, one church, or is found only in one "special", concentrated place. The Light is always being born anew, always renewing itself, always unfolding and expressing itself through us and through others. No one has more of it, nor does anyone have less of it. Enlightened teachers have revealed it; lay persons around the world give evidence of it throughout their lives and activities. If Jesus' teaching is true, "Ye are the light of the world", that truth applies equally to all people regardless of race, creed or credentials!

The miracle of Christmas is, then, that we are, each one of us renewed again in our hearts, souls and spirits in the light. We are reminded of this anew in the splendor of Handel's "Messiah". We are reminded in the whispering winds echoing that first angel choir announcing Jesus' birth. We are reminded that the *Light* is born anew and that each of us is the demonstration and the demonstrator!

Yes, we are newly reminded this festive holiday, with all of its tinsel and trimmings and graced with gentleness in children and adults, in friends and strangers alike, that Christ is reborn in our hearts, our lives, our hopes and our dreams.

And if we pause long enough, amidst the busy-ness of our lives and/or the merriment of the season, the warmth of the Christ love will touch our hearts, heal our wounds and allow our Inner Light to shine forth, to glorify our Father (Source) which is in heaven (within).

49

The Transforming Power of Love

In considering the holidays ahead, I am reminded of Charles Dickens much beloved *A Christmas Carol* in which the central character, Ebenezer Scrooge, is visited by three spirits: The Spirit of Christmas Past, the Spirit of Christmas Present and the Spirit of Christmas To Come. The setting is Christmas Eve in London, England.

The theme of Dickens' story relates how Mr. Scrooge has reacted to the twists of his life and how he has been affected by his past. The Spirit of Christmas Past reviews the painful memories and tragic experiences that shaped and molded him, that have helped to create the picture of him as a man of limited vision, anger, hurt, selfishness and much attachment to worldly goods as his only real security in life.

As the story moves on, Scrooge is visited by another being, the Spirit of Christmas Present. Here we see what is currently in store for him amongst his family and among what few associates and acquaintances he has left. The portrait is dismal. Because of his past actions, his family (a nephew with children) does not look forward to welcoming him into their holiday gathering. Nor does anyone else ask for him or express concern or any love for him.

In the last visitation by the Spirit of Christmas Yet To Come, he is shown a preview of his death—a bleak, empty picture of a man forgotten. No friends or family come to pay homage to his memory. His possessions are picked over by strangers who have no kind or loving feelings for him. He is given to understand that not even his nephew knows or can come to claim his body.

The Spirit of Christmas To Come then suggests an alternative picture—that he, Scrooge, yet has a choice he can make. His future can be different; his experience of himself can be renewed, even forgiven, released and ultimately transformed.

He is shown that in order to change the harsh coldness and stark, severe image of the future, he can heal himself by loving—reaching out to his nephew and his family and the people who are a part of his life. Only then can he experience the promise of life, the fullness that comes from giving and sharing.

The message of *A Christmas Carol* is a powerful metaphor for our growth and celebration of life, not only at this holiday season, but for all time.

As we review the frustrations, the hurts and disappointments in our past, we are reminded that merely glossing over them or burying them is not enough. We must make a conscious effort to forgive those who have wronged us, to release those experiences which have set in motion the wheels of life that bring us to the present. We must stop denying our Divine Nature!

In accepting our Divine Essence, we accept that the present can be changed, not held as a bondage over our being creating a limited and restricted life. The present, then, is a wonderful opportunity to learn from each event and each person that our life can be different. We do have choice!

As the realization grows within us that our future is not fixed by some unchangeable fate, but that we can create a very exciting and different experience for ourselves and thus affect the quality of life around us and our loved ones, the image of our personal future is one in which love, peace and all the fullness that life can offer is available to each of us.

In part, the message of Dickens' story, *A Christmas Carol*, is to release *all* of our past through the transformation of love—accepting ourselves in the here and now so that we can be effective, progressive and unlimited in consciousness. It also speaks to the deeper Inner Nature that suggests that we can always choose to change, at any moment, whatever is limited, or limiting in our lives.

"God bless us, everyone!"

50

The Diadem of Spirit

"But as it is written, eye hath not seen, nor ear heard, neither have entered into the heart of man, the things that God hath prepared for them that love Him."

1 Corinthians 2:9

∾

Perhaps one of, if not the most profound and significant messages of Christmas is the overwhelming theme of love. There is no other time of year more intently focused upon the implications of love or its broadest ramifications for the effective living of our spiritual as well as our daily life!

Ancient traditions, enlightenment teachers and modern mystics agree that our deepest mission is to become awake, or aware of our Sacred Essence. To "awaken" is to consciously know or learn how to become at one with (attuned to) this Divine Spark! When and as we gradually awaken to the fullness of our potential, or our Divine Nature, we gradually come to experience, learn the meaning of and discover totally the deepest essence of love in all of its radiant splendor, majesty and magnificence.

"Eye hath not seen, nor ear heard, neither have entered into the heart of man ..." Metaphysically speaking, this suggests that not what we have seen or heard through our senses, (or through our physical, sexual, emotional, mental and psychological experiences), nor what we may think we have "seen" or "heard" (been made aware of) through the eyes of others or through the teachings of others is to be compared to what is yet to be revealed to us! Think of it! Whatever life has brought us so far pales when we begin to allow ourselves to discover the unlimited abundance, revelation and depth of our greater being through allowing our Holy and Sacred Essence to emerge in our lives.

"... neither have entered into the heart of man ..." Here is a phrase that might mean many things. Could it suggest that all of the emotions, feelings, so-called spiritual "highs", revelations or insights that we may have had are not yet to be compared to what awaits us? Perhaps. Might it not also imply that whatever stage of growth (i.e., level of awareness) we are upon, there is always more? And perchance, also, that our egoic nature clouds our inner (spiritual) heart and we cannot, therefore, "see" or "hear" clearly?

Spiritual teachers the world over consistently say that strongly placed or fixed attachments (such as guilt, fear, unresolved hurt or conflict, unforgiving attitudes, unyielding viewpoints, possessiveness about things, places or people in our lives) prevent us from experiencing the deep things of God. They block a closer connection to our real heritage, our divine nature. Yet, we can lose these restrictive aspects of our nature by choosing to see them anew through the eyes and ears of love, or through forgiveness, release and changing our beliefs about ourselves!

"... the things that God hath prepared for them that love Him." Here we might come to begin to know the fullness, the richness of life in such ways as inner healing, freedom from stress, overcoming restrictive habits, transforming relationships, developing talents, opening to new opportunities and allowing our lives to be sources of consistent deepening in all areas that are meaningful, useful and practical!

What then is God's Love? How do we attain it? How can we individually recognize it?

(1) God's Love is already ours! It is a gift. We do not earn it. We do not buy it, trade for it, beg for it, cajole or wheedle the Supreme Being for it. We cannot bargain with God to gain access to that unlimited Love which comes from the Source. It is already ours! All we need do is to accept it, unconditionally, without limit or restraint!

(2) Surrender our ego sense. This step is also called yielding or releasing our ego (emotionally) backed demands (attachments) or perceptions that interfere with God's Love or Presence in our lives. Surrender implies a shifting in our lives to give the deepest, innermost part of our nature an avenue to surface or emerge. When we let go of our ego demands, then our spiritual eyes and ears become receptive, open and clear. We see inwardly, we hear inwardly the Voice of the Presence. When we begin to realize that the love we've been seeking externally is only a reflection, a tiny spark of the Larger Love, the Divine Flame, unbelievable transformation occurs in us and in our lives.

(3) Affirm God's Presence in our life by giving Him first place in all our affairs. On a realistic, day to day basis, this means being willing to choose experiences which uplift, inspire, ennoble and enrich our life. It is not enough to think about being loving toward ourselves and toward others; we must consciously and conscientiously choose to act out of love in all areas of our life. At work or at play, at home or away, the Source of Life is our reason for being. When we act out of love, we are kind, forbearing, hopeful, peaceful, harmonious and filled with joy and thanksgiving.

Perhaps then, this is what is meant when Paul said to the Corinthians that God has substance for us, already prepared for us, as we honor (accept) God's gifts to us.

The real diadem (crown), multifaceted dimensions of Spirit is discovered as we consistently take charge of our own life. To take charge signifies a shifting away from blame, hurt and fear to the conscious use of the love principle in our lives.. As stated at the beginning, love is one of the overwhelming themes of Christmas. Let us allow Christmas its emergence as a gentle reminder of the possibilities that are always available to each of us. The holiday season affords us numerous opportunities to give, to share and blend our individual and collective efforts to demonstrate the principle of love. In so doing, we become open to, receptive to the incredible promise of our text: *"But as it is written, eye hath not seen, nor ear heard, neither have entered into the heart of man, the things that God hath prepared for them that Love Him."*

51

Living the Miracle of Christmas

"I am come that you might have life, and have it more abundantly." **John 10:10**

"I know, that, for the right practice of it, the heart must be empty of all else; because God wills to possess the heart alone; and as He cannot possess it alone unless it is empty of all else, so He cannot work in it what He would unless it be left vacant for Him."
Brother Lawrence

∾

Christmas! Images of children singing carols, families and friends gathering, gala celebrations, candle lighted churches, gaily decorated trees and homes and stores alike flood the memory and stimulate the senses. It's a season of reminiscing, of recapturing traditions and creating new experiences. It's a time that stirs the heart and moves the spirit as we seek to blend the old traditions with the fast paced movement toward the new. Christmas is more a time of the heart, perhaps, than almost any other season of the year.

For many people, however, Christmas is not a season of joy or cause for celebration. Rather, it's a time when those who are alone, or alone and elderly feel alienated, hurt and separate. Poor people often are unable to experience any change of heart, mind or consciousness because of the restrictions of conditions that bind them. The sick and dying in many instances feel hopeless or frightened or confused about their whole purpose in life. There is no joy in Christmas then. It is but an emphasis of life's hurts and rejection.

How can we, in the midst of holiday shopping, Christmas parties and festivities and celebrations of every kind on the one hand, as contrasted by fear, loneliness, depression and despair on the other hand—help to create a valid experience of "Living the Miracle of Christmas", first of all for ourselves and then, perhaps, for others?

The Miracle of Christmas begins in Holy Scripture, which tells of the virgin birth of Jesus the Christ, and the singular effect that birth nearly 2000 years ago has had upon mankind. His life so captures the spirit, so fires the imagination and stirs the heart that 19 centuries later we are still attempting to comprehend and open our minds, nay our very being to the unfathomable mystery contained in the life and teachings of that One Solitary Life!

Living the Miracle of Christmas is about sharing, being open, receptive and aligned to the Eternal Presence wherever we are, whoever and whatever we are, and whatever we are doing—anytime! In Living the Miracle, we are ever sensitive to our own Higher Self and its subtle, loving guidance as it emerges in our life. We express patience with all other people as that guidance emerges for them from their own Higher Selves.

Living means to *actively, consciously participate* in the flow of life around and about us. It suggests involvement and interest in a responsible manner, with ourselves, other people, our community, and thus with life in its largest sense. Living implies interacting with or becoming aware of the varied, kaleidoscopic landscape of our inner and outer nature to enable us to participate fully in the expression. Christmas is not an event or something that happens to us at a certain time of the calendar year. Christmas is an experience of conscious involvement with life and the nature of that miracle every day.

Living the ***Miracle*** of Christmas suggests profound sensitivity to and appreciation of the wonder this holiday symbolizes. When the exquisite strains of Handel's *Messiah* fall upon our ears and we enter the realms of that glorious, majestic, stirring music, we enter for a moment, an hour, or perhaps for an evening the transcendent dimensions and "hear" the song of angels in our heart.

On another level, we are experiencing the meaning and miracle of Christmas, indeed, when we remember loved ones or friends and share tokens of ourselves with presents that result in misty (love overflowing) eyes, broad grins, warmth and laughter. And, yes, we live the miracle of Christmas when we reach out by telephone, by letters or cards, when we send flowers or a Christmas basket of fruit, or when we visit the sick or grieving, or forlorn or lonely, and feel the warm clasp of their hands in ours, their kiss upon our cheek, or their heartfelt "thank you" in their tender embrace. This is the heart of Christmas.

A very important and powerful message of Christmas is expressed in the consciousness of the celebrants. Even if only for the duration of the season, men, women and children around the world express one of the deeper meanings of Christmas in loving actions, kindness and gentleness. People stop to greet each other warmly. They go out of their way to do a favor expressing tenderness, caring and nurturing. For a brief time "swords are sheathed", grievances are forgotten, and longstanding hurts are forgiven. Such simple yet profound actions are evidence that we can live the miracle of Christmas.

The real challenge of Living the Miracle of Christmas emerges as we try to remember to create a loving place in our hearts for the reembodiment of the Lord Christ as a Presence in consciousness in our lives every day of every year! Remembering is the subtle call of spirit to love instead of hate, to hope instead of despairing, to trust instead of fearing, to give and be joyful instead of hurting. We Live the Miracle of Christmas daily as we honor the truth of who we are in our thoughts, words, deeds and activities and thus become a living example of Jesus' teaching, "I am come that you might have life, and have it more abundantly."

52

Rejoice in His Wondrous Gifts

"The gift of heaven is Life and not Death; Love and not Hate; Peace and not Confusion. And we enter into this paradise through the gateway of love toward one another and toward God..."

Ernest Holmes
Science of Mind

∾

The most precious gift we have is that of our life. At this season of the year, we have many opportunities to help remind us of what our lives are reflecting or signifying. It is a time to "sum up the year" with various celebrations, give presents to loved ones and gather friends around us for moments permeated with warmth and meaning.

In many instances, however, there is confusion instead of peace, hurt instead of love, death instead of life. Looking back over the past year, we discover here and there broken relationships that are still causing conflicting feelings; jobs that have terminated and no new ones have yet appeared; death has taken loved ones and no others seem able to fill the void. Finances may be low or almost nonexistent and no way has yet appeared to increase prosperity. When personally faced with such conflicts and distresses, how can we deny appearances to accept that our life is indeed a gift?

Spiritual teachings have long affirmed that in order to become open to the power of God, we must first *accept* that it is available to us.

Crisis in our lives often creates an inner state that permits us to become receptive or open to the Presence of God in sometimes striking and unexpected ways. The following life-changing experience shared by a business man suggests the use of prayer as a way to create that acceptance or openness.

"I was reading a book. The house was quiet and the family had retired. It was a stressful time in my life and I had been putting more time than usual into prayer. Suddenly the room became bright, then brighter, as though some great source of light had been turned on and was filling the space all around me and my mind and my body. It was overwhelming. I was stunned. It lasted only about a half hour, but it gave me a sense of the holy that has never left me in twenty-two years. It took away my fear of death. It gave me absolute certitude that God exists."

When we are in pain or conflict, it is difficult to find meaning in our current circumstances. Yet, again the spiritual teachings suggest that we must turn away from lack, fear and limitation and grasp the very hand of God. We do this when we make a *conscious choice* to begin moving in the direction of desired change. Conflict pulls at and impairs our focus. It scatters our thoughts. It paralyzes our efforts to mobilize our forces for change.

Choice implies a specific focus of energy. In prayer, we seek a connection with God that assures us we are not separate from the Source, that we can be alone but not lonely—that we can ache, feel hurt and loss, but not become caught in the appearances of lack or limitation.

When we make a conscious choice to grow, or move beyond the turbulence of the moment, we engage the full, deeper, inner powers of our being and thus that larger connection with the Universe to aid, strengthen, inspire, encourage, uplift and empower us. Such a choice moves us in the direction of "...Life and not Death; Love and not Hate; Peace and not Confusion."

At this time of year when so many greetings of good will are exchanged around the world, rejoicing in His Presence will be more meaningful if we can first honor and thus accept the challenges that our life is providing through our experiences.

The wondrous gifts of the Christ, of the Source of Life are ours the very moment we give thanks for them and accept them. Our good is awaiting us! It is already appearing in our world. Our choice is to accept it and to continue to praise and give thanks for it. This places us in resonance with the transcendent fields of Pure Being. As we do this more and more, our consciousness moves into deeper and more profound fullness. We enter this paradise through the gateway of love toward one another and toward God. Remember an ancient proverb, "The longest journey begins with the first step."

The words of a favorite poet come to mind:

The angels keep their ancient places;
Turn but a stone and start a wing!
'Tis ye, 'tis your estranged faces,
That miss the many splendored thing.

Francis Thompson
In No Strange Land